JOSEPHINE BUTLER—
THE FORGOTTEN SAINT

JOSEPHINE BUTLER—
THE FORGOTTEN SAINT

JOSEPH WILLIAMSON

Joseph Williamson

HIGH SPRAY
29 MARINE DRIVE WEST
WEST WITTERING
CHICHESTER
SUSSEX PO20 8HH

THE FAITH PRESS
Leighton Buzzard, Beds. LU7 7NQ

First published in 1977
© *Joseph Williamson, 1977*

PRINTED IN GREAT BRITAIN
in 10pt. Times Roman type
BY THE FAITH PRESS LTD.
LEIGHTON BUZZARD, BEDS. LU7 7NQ
ISBN 07164 0485 0

Contents

	Page
FOREWORD	7
PREFACE	9
CHAPTER 1	13
,, 2	20
,, 3	29
,, 4	41
,, 5	51
,, 6	58
,, 7	70
,, 8	77
,, 9	85
,, 10	91
,, 11	109
EPILOGUE	120
BIBLIOGRAPHY	122

TO MARY

Foreword

ALL lovers of truth and justice must be deeply grateful to the Reverend Joseph Williamson for his unsurpassed understanding of Josephine Butler's real character, and for his unselfed motive in writing this book about her.

His thinking is akin to hers and he can understand her high ideals, saintliness, heroism and divine inspiration.

Josephine Butler was my grandmother. As a child I used to visit her and I loved going to see her. She was so kind to children and made them feel happy. I can still remember her fine features, her lace cap with its mauve ribbons, and the warm rich sound of her voice.

Some of those who had seen her and heard her speak from a platform told me that it was impossible to believe that anyone *could* look more beautiful and also that the tone of her voice was unforgettable.

She dressed with great taste; she had wit and humour and could say very funny things. She was a fine and fearless rider who could impart confidence to a nervous horse.

I have been told by those who heard her play that she was an extremely good musician and played with great feeling. Some of her friends presented her with the Broadwood Grand piano which won the first prize at the Great Exhibition of 1851, when Jenny Lind sang to it accompanied by Sterndale Bennett, from whom Josephine had some lessons. She said that no other piano responded to her touch so well as this one.

Josephine had a more than merely amateur gift for drawing and painting, her work was accurate and charmingly coloured. She had an innate sense of beauty.

JOSEPHINE BUTLER—THE FORGOTTEN SAINT

I quote from Professor James Stuart who knew Mrs. Butler and helped her with her work—

'And now what is the sum of it all? It seems to me to be this, that we must all be glad that she lived. We are each of us individually better, and the world as a whole is better, because she lived; and the seed that she has sown can never die.'

Hetha Butler
24th September 1976

Preface

AS I approach this attempt to place Josephine Butler where I think she deserves to be in relation to English Christian history, I can find no words too superlative to describe her greatness.

Coming as I do from the lowest rung of the class ladder, I believe I am qualified to judge the true value of dedicated culture. I felt the touch of this dedication from priests and Christian women in the slums of London's East End at the turn of the century, and for years afterwards, in conditions of want, ignorance and the deepest poverty. Experience counts for a good deal.

In my early youth I believed that the conditions of mankind were fixed and that the gentry, which meant the educated and fortunate ones, were meant to be on top. Such a thing as privilege did not occur to me. In the words of the well-known hymn:

> The rich man in his castle,
> The poor man at his gate,
> God made them, high or lowly,
> And ordered their estate.

The people who worked in the slums were looked on by us as very close to gods. My mother would say: 'He's a gentleman. She's a lady', and it meant the same as being a saint, for they could have stayed away from us and didn't. That is how the poor and prostitute girls looked upon Josephine Butler when she visited them in the Liverpool workhouse and sat with them on the stone floor.

I see Josephine in the setting of my own special call, for

it was not until a year or two after I had started to make a way of escape for prostitutes in Stepney that I first learned of her existence. An old lady in Liverpool sent me a booklet with an accompanying letter which said, 'You must read about Josephine Butler'. At the time, I put down my lack of knowledge about her to my own general ignorance. But later, in my talks at universities and in towns and schools up and down the country, when I asked for the names of the really great women of the last century, I found that no one else seemed to have heard of her. Even among the most learned and widely read I discovered the same dull ignorance.

So I do not ask to be forgiven for calling Josephine Butler the Forgotten Saint. For saint she is.

I make no apology for writing so little of my own and for quoting so much of the actual words of Josephine Butler. To let her speak is to feast on the beauty of words spoken by one inspired by God; by one who gives her whole self to her project, which would seem to be out of the range of a woman living in the last century. Let her speak and let us listen and heed.

Through the kindness of my wife I was driven to Northumbria where we visited the scenes of Josephine's youth, including Devil Water and the woods where she received her call and wrestled with God. The highlight of the journey was meeting Miss Hetha Butler at Wooler. To meet the granddaughter of Josephine was a joy, and meant also seeing and reading treasures of her grandmother whom she knew personally as a child. Miss Butler not only read the script of my modest tribute to Josephine but honoured my effort by writing the Foreword, for which I am most grateful.

Mrs. Coggan was kind enough to read my script also and to make suggestions. She encouraged me by saying:

'You have drawn out a splendid portrait of a sensitive and courageous woman. You have shown her marvellous patience alongside her enthusiasm; her realism alongside her optimism. Undergirding all her life and work you have so well stressed her trust in God and her dependence on prayer.'

My thanks to the authors I quote for their indulgence, especially to Glen Petrie and to his publisher Macmillan, London Ltd. for allowing me to quote passages from *A Singular Iniquity*.

I am most grateful to Miss Myrtle Powley for her planning of the book and for her expert touches.

Finally to my wife goes love and thanks; she has typed and read with superb and untiring patience.

Joseph Williamson

Chapter 1

JOSEPHINE GREY was born in 1828, in the border country of Northumberland. Hers was a famous family which for generations had given prominent service to the nation. Her father was John Grey, a god-fearing man and a firm opponent of the slave trade, who shared his liberal ideas with his family. Thus, though in many respects her upbringing was a sheltered one, in a wealthy home far removed from cities with their attendant evils, Josephine was early made aware of the existence of social wrongs. She once wrote, of her girlhood: 'It was my lot to be haunted by the problems which present themselves to every thoughtful mind.' This preoccupation increased year after year. She records how, as in a vision, she saw some of the saddest miseries on earth, injustices and cruelties, 'practised by man on man and by man on woman'.

At seventeen, she underwent a darkness of the soul which endured for a whole year. Looking back, she saw it as sent by God, whose name, she had learned, was Love. At the time, her response to Him was one of dread: 'I fled from Him.'

At other times she would call out in her agony: 'Who are you? Where are you?' She was obsessed with the question of why people should suffer.

She records: 'I fought the battle alone in deep recesses of beautiful woods and pine forests around our home.' For hours, days, weeks she haunted these retreats, seeking an answer to her soul's trouble. It seemed that 'the end must have been defeat and death had not the Saviour imparted to the child wrestler something of the virtue of His own midnight agony'. The fight was renewed, but now there was light and hope. The determination to seek and knock became 'an anchor of the soul'.

I myself have spent hours in those woodlands and under those trees trying to recapture Josephine's spirit and faith. It was there that, at last, she looked her Liberator in the face, standing at the side of 'the woman who was a sinner in the city'. She wrote: 'He can also say of me: "This woman has not ceased to kiss My feet." '

Josephine was no ordinary girl and maybe her father did not fully realise the depth of her sensitive nature. He would have been very disturbed indeed had he known what was going on, for a whole year, in his child's mind, and because she was a girl, it would have distressed him even more. His daughter had developed not only a woman's tenderness, as befitted a woman of her station and upbringing; she had a scholar's brain. Both were to be of intense value to her in her future vocation.

Josephine married George Butler on January 8th 1852. His letters to her before their marriage show his awareness and deep understanding of her special qualities. 'I must not suffer myself to be dazzled, or to fancy that I have within me that power of judging and acting aright which would alone authorise me to point out to you any path in which you ought to walk. I am content to leave you to walk by yourself in the path you shall choose; but I know that I do not leave you alone and unsupported for His arm will guide, strengthen and protect you.'

This was not the passing zeal of a keen lover. It was a lasting promise. In later years, George was often to be both mother and father to their children, and to carry much of the supporting weight of his wife's brave and often dangerous campaign.

The Butlers spent five busy and happy years at Oxford, where George was Examiner to the University. Josephine enjoyed the academic life and was fully able to join in the stimulating conversation. As an educationist, George was considerably in advance of his time. One of his innovations was the introduction into the university of the study of Geography, a subject previously thought fit only for elementary boys' schools. Josephine delighted in assisting him in mapmaking, and related with relish an incident when a certain college tutor was unable to locate Egypt on a map.

Oxford had its pleasant side, but for Josephine there were dark aspects too. She had moved from the freedom of life in the country to a university town with its male-dominated society. Most of the scholars were celibates. There were few women in the place, and therefore little family life. Often Josephine was the only woman present at a social gathering. She listened to the men's conversation with a sore heart. On one occasion the discussion turned on a recently published book by Mrs. Gaskell, *Ruth,* whose heroine, a seventeen-year-old seamstress, was seduced by a young gentleman and left to struggle to bring up her child. Josephine felt that the judgements passed by the men in the company were utterly false. 'A moral lapse in a woman was spoken of as an immensely worse thing than in a man; with no comparison between them.'

A pure woman was expected to be ignorant of a certain class of evil. Josephine was distressed to learn of the plight of a young girl who had been wronged and deserted by a man held in high regard in the university. She ventured to approach one of the wisest men in the university, whom she believed to be sincerely Christian, in the hope that he might help to bring the man concerned to a sense of his wrongdoing. His reply distressed her. It could do nothing but harm, he protested, to open up a question such as this. It would be dangerous to arouse a sleeping lion. Josephine was sickened. She recalled the terrible prophetic words of the poet Blake:

> The harlot's curse from street to street
> Shall weave old England's winding sheet.

Here in Oxford, in 1853, Josephine tells us: 'Every instinct of womanhood within me was already in revolt against certain accepted theories in society, and I suffered as only God and the faithful companion of my life could ever know.'

About that time certain publicity was given to the case of a young mother, sent to Newgate for the murder of her infant 'whose father, under cover of the death-like silence prescribed by Oxford philosophers—a silence which is in fact a permanent endorsement of injustice—had perjured himself to her, had forsaken and forgotten her, and fallen back, with no accusing conscience, on his easy social life, and possibly his academic honours.' Josephine wanted to visit the girl in Newgate, but George restrained her, suggesting that he should write to the prison chaplain and ask him to send the girl to them when the sentence expired. In due course she came to live in their home, 'the first of the world of unhappy women of humble class whom he welcomed to his own home. She was not the last.'

Pondering these evils, in a vision Josephine heard the sound of 'a woman aspiring to heaven and dragged back to hell' and 'my heart was pierced with pain'. At the evening gatherings of the highly educated masculine world she resolved to hold her peace—'to speak little with men but much with God'.

George largely shared his wife's view of academic society. For all their scholarship, these men had one-sided opinions. At first, Josephine had rather exaggerated their wisdom, so that she was surprised when George would say, 'I am rather sorry for so-and-so.' It was rather like saying, 'I am rather sorry for Solomon.' 'They know no better, poor fellows,' George would say to her consolingly, and she began to regard this home of learning and intellect in a new light. She clearly adored her husband. 'Besides all he was in himself and all the work he did, he was of a character to be able from the first to correct the judgement and soothe the spirit of the companion of his life when "the waters had come even unto her soul" . . . and I want to show that he was even more to me in later life than a wise and noble supporter in the work which may have been called more especially my own. But for him I should have been more perplexed; the idea of equality between the sexes, and the responsibility of all human beings to the moral law, seems to have been instinctive in him.'

The secret that made George and Josephine such a perfect team was their simple and utter dependence upon God. In their marriage they were a long way ahead of their time. In an age when the man's dominance over the wife was unquestioned, George laid down for himself marriage on equal terms, and he suffered for it at the hands of society. Throughout their lives, he and Josephine faced their problems together, and God was their tribunal.

It was illness, and the orders of a medical specialist from London, that eventually forced Josephine to leave Oxford. In 1856 she spent several months with their children in Northumberland where George wrote to her: 'I am grieved to hear of your sufferings but you write so cheerfully, and express such a loving confidence in One who is able to heal all our sicknesses. However sad at heart I may sometimes feel about you, I will try to bring myself face to face with those mighty promises which are held out to those who "rest in the Lord and wait patiently upon Him". And then I hope we shall still be able to go hand in hand in our work on earth.'

In the autumn of 1857, George accepted the post of vice-principal of Cheltenham College, where he remained until 1865. In August 1864 their little daughter Eva, who had never had a day's illness, sprang from her bed to greet her parents as they returned from an engagement. She ran to the banisters, overbalanced and crashed to the stone floor. She died within an hour.

They were shaken out of the pain and gloom following her death by their second son, Stanley, becoming very ill with diphtheria. When he had recovered, Josephine took him on a visit to her niece in Genoa. From there, they were to go by boat to Naples, home of Josephine's favourite sister Harriet Meuricoffre, but Josephine became so ill that she was put ashore at Leghorn.

In the winter of 1865, George was offered the principalship of Liverpool College. So in January 1866, the family moved once again. George and the three boys went daily to the College and Josephine was left for hours alone and ached for Eva. She wrote: 'I became possessed with an irresistible desire to go forth and find some pain keener than my own, to meet with people more unhappy than myself (for I knew there were thousands of such). I did not exaggerate my own trial. . . . My sole wish was to plunge into the heart of some human misery and to say to afflicted people: I too have suffered.'

It was not difficult to find misery in Liverpool. She was drawn to the workhouse which then contained five thousand persons. The general hospital for paupers was then under the beneficent control of Agnes Johns. But other departments were not given so much care. 'There was on the ground floor a Bridewell for women, consisting of huge cellars, bare and unfurnished, with damp stone floors. These were called the "oakum sheds", and to these came voluntarily creatures driven by hunger, destitution or vice, begging for a few nights' shelter and a piece of bread, in return for which they picked their allotted portion of oakum. Others were sent there as prisoners.'

Josephine begged admission to the gloomy vault crowded with more than two hundred women and girls. She sat on the floor among them and picked oakum. They laughed at her, 'but while we laughed we became friends'. Some jeered at this fine lady who would return home to her grand house and good food. But Josephine persevered in winning their friendship. She encouraged the women to pray with her. One tall, handsome girl recited the fourteenth chapter of St John's Gospel, ending with the words, 'Peace I leave with you. My peace I give unto you. Let not your heart be troubled, neither let it be afraid.' She had selected the passage herself. Josephine records: 'She had prepared the way for me, and I said, "Now let us all kneel, and cry to that same Jesus who spoke those words."'

Josephine Butler's scholarly ability attracted attention in educational circles. So we find the great pioneer for the education of women, Miss Clough, calling one day in 1867 'to ascertain the state of mind of the Principal of Liverpool College in regard to the beautiful schemes which were even then taking shape in her fruitful brain for the benefit of her fellow-women.' That visit led to the formation of the North of England Council for Promoting the Higher Education for Women, made up largely of schoolmistresses in several large northern towns. Josephine was President of this council from 1867-1873. She was an active President and did much to influence the academics of Cambridge on a special visit there. Forty-eight undergraduates requested private interviews with her, and she talked to many of the senior men, including one elderly don who told her, with tears in his eyes, 'I fear we get selfish here, and forget how much there is of sorrow in the world outside us.'

How well Josephine could have continued her work with the North of England Council! With her gifts and personality she could, one feels, have forged all the necessary links to gain, at least for women of the upper and middle classes, recognition in the universities and acknowledgement of their scholarly abilities. Furthermore, the work would have suited her, allowing full use of her gifts. She would meet intellects equal to her own, and the many dinner parties and conferences she was called upon to attend offered her unlimited scope for spreading her ideas. Many writers have claimed that it was a pity she left the educational field. But already more pressing interests were claiming her attention.

Chapter 2

IN 1864, unknown to Josephine as to most people, including possibly many MPs, there was passed in Parliament a temporary Act 'for the prevention of contagious diseases at certain naval and military stations'. This Act aimed to bring in a system already established in most countries of Europe, to prevent the spread of venereal disease by the establishment of official brothels where the women would be under medical supervision. Women suspected of being prostitutes would be officially registered by the police and regularly examined for the incidence of disease. The Act was renewed in 1866 and further extended to eighteen towns in 1869. (We do well to note that today, in 1977, men are publicly advocating the setting up of similar establishments in special areas in several of our cities.)

When she learned of the existence of the Acts, it came as a great shock to Josephine and changed her whole life. She was quick to recognise the abuses which could result. Completely innocent women and young girls were liable to arrest at the whim of a corrupt policeman, or following the receipt of false information, and subjected to the most painful and humiliating surgical examination. A woman, however innocent or repentant, once branded as a prostitute, had no hope of making a respectable life for herself, as a result of the Acts. Thus many women found themselves forced into prostitution since, once placed on the police register, nobody would wish to give them other employment.

Though tormented by feelings of trepidation, Josephine felt an irresistible call to fight against this legislation. She revealed in a speech in which she told of her call:

'I first became acquainted with this system as it existed in Paris. I was one of those persons—they were few, I believe —who read that very brief debate in the House of Commons in 1866, when Mr. Henley and Mr. Ayrton alone, but clearly and boldly, entered their protest. It was in that year that the knowledge first broke upon me that this system, which I had so long regarded with horror, had actually found a footing in our England. It seemed to me as if a dark cloud were hanging in the horizon, threatening our land. The depression which took possession of my mind was overwhelming. A few days ago I found a record of those days in an old manuscript book long laid aside. In turning over its leaves I found a note of that debate in the House, the date, and a written expression, which I had since forgotten, of a presentiment which at that time filled my mind, that in some way or another I should be called to meet this evil thing face to face—a trembling presentiment, which I could not escape from, that, do what I would, I myself must enter into this cloud. I find there recorded also a brief prayer *beseeching that if I MUST descend into darkness, that divine hand, whose touch is health and strength, would hold mine fast in the darkness.* I can recollect going out into the garden, hoping that the sight of the flowers and blue sky might banish the mental pain; but it clung too fast for a time for any outward impression to remove it, and I envied the sparrows upon the garden walk because they had not minds and souls capable of torment like mine. But NOW, when I look back, I see that the prayer has been heard, the divine hand has held mine, often when I knew it not. And friends, God can give more than power to bear the pain; there is a positive *joy* in His service, and in any warfare in which He, who conquered sin and death and hell, goes before us and is our reward.

'The appeal to take up this cause reached me first from a group of medical men, who had for some time been making strenuous efforts to prevent the introduction in our land of the principle of regulation by the State of the social evil. The experience gained during their efforts had convinced them that in order to be successful they must summon to their aid forces far beyond the arguments, strong as these were, based on physiological scientific grounds. They recognised that the persons most insulted by the Napoleonic system with which our legislators of that day had become enamoured, being women, these women must find representatives of their own sex to protest against and to claim a practical repentance from the Parliament and the Government which had flung this insult in their face.

' "It was on landing at Dover from our delightful summer tour in 1869 that we first learned that a small clique in Parliament had been too successfully busy over this week of darkness during the hot August days or rather nights, in a thin House, in which most of those present were but vaguely cognisant of the meaning and purpose of the proposed constitutional change."

'During the three months which followed this communication I was very unhappy. I can only give a very imperfect impression of the sufferings of that time. The toils and conflicts of the years that followed were light in comparison with the anguish of that first plunge into the full realisation of the villainy there is in the world, and the dread of being called to oppose it. Like Jonah when he was charged by God with a Commission which he could not endure to contemplate, "I fled from the face of the Lord". I worked hard at other things—good works as I thought—with a kind of half conscious hope that God would accept THAT work and not require me to go further and run my heart against that naked sword which seemed to be held out. But the hand of the Lord was upon me; night and day the pressure increased. From an old manuscript book in which I sometimes wrote, I quote the following: "Sept 1869 'Now is your hour and the power of darkness'. O Christ if Thy Spirit fainted in that hour how can mine sustain it? It is now many weeks since I knew that Parliament had sanctioned this great wickedness and I have not put on my armour, nor am I yet ready. Nothing so wears me out, body and soul, as anger, fruitless anger; and this thing fills me with such an anger, and even hatred that I fear to face it. The thought of this atrocity kills charity and hinders my prayers. But there is surely a way of being angry without sin. I pray Thee O God, to give me a deep, well governed and lifelong hatred of all such injustice, tyranny and cruelty; and at the same time give me that divine compassion which is willing to live and suffer long for love of souls, or to fling itself into the breach and die at once. This is perhaps after all the very work, the very mission, I longed for years ago, and saw coming, afar off, like a bright star. But seen near as it approaches, it is so dreadful, so difficult, so disgusting, that I tremble to look at it; and it is hard to see and know whether or not God is indeed calling me concerning it. If doubt were gone and I felt sure He means me to rise in revolt and rebellion (for that it must be) against men, even against our rulers, then I would do it with zeal, however repulsive to others may seem the task." '

Now Josephine had further to test the loyalty and understanding spirit of her husband. She knew that the awful nature of her call would bring unpopularity to herself and suffering to George. Few, if any, of their own class and associates would understand. Her work would involve being away from home a great deal and facing bitter opposition at every turn. She had not only to find supporters, she had to face the enmity of Parliament itself. How then was she to tell George?

'I went to him one evening when he was alone, all the household having gone to rest. At his study I hesitated and leaned my cheek against his door; and as I leaned I prayed. Then I went in and gave him something I had written, and left him. I did not see him until the next day. He looked pale and troubled, and for some days was silent. But by and by we spoke together about it freely and we agreed together that we must move in the matter and that an appeal must be made to the people. (Already many members of both Houses of Parliament, bishops and responsible officials had been appealed to, but so far in vain.) I spoke to my husband then of all that was in my mind, and said, "I feel as if I must go out into the streets and CRY ALOUD, or my heart will break".... His whole attitude in response to my words cited above expressed, "Go! and God be with you".'

Josephine's first public meeting was in Crewe, at the Mechanics' Institute, where she addressed a gathering of workmen from the locomotive sheds, after working hours. Afterwards some of the men told her:

'We understand you perfectly. We in this group served an apprenticeship in Paris, and we have seen and know for ourselves the truth of what you say. We have said to each other that it would be the death-knell of the moral life of England were she to copy France in this matter.'

From Crewe, she went to Leeds, York, Sunderland and Newcastle-on-Tyne. Within three weeks, more mass meetings were arranged. Meanwhile the Ladies National Association for the Repeal of the Contagious Diseases Acts had been formed towards the end of 1869. They published a solemn protest, Josephine's name heading the first list of 220 names attached to it. It shows her influence in every clause:

'We the undersigned, enter our solemn protest against these Acts.

(1) Because, involving as they do such a momentous change in legal safeguards hitherto enjoyed by women in common with men, they have been passed not only without the knowledge of the country, but unknown in a great measure to Parliament itself; and we hold that neither the Representatives of the People nor the Press fulfil the duties

which are expected of them, when they allow such legislation to take place without the fullest discussion.

(2) Because, so far as women are concerned, they remove every guarantee of personal security which the law has established and held sacred, and put their reputation, their freedom, and their persons absolutely in the power of the police.

(3) Because the law is bound, in any country professing to give civil liberty to its subjects, to define clearly an offence which it punishes.

(4) Because it is unjust to punish the sex who are the victims of a vice, and leave unpunished the sex who are the main cause of the vice and its dreaded consequences; and we consider that liability to arrest, forced medical treatment, and (where this is resisted) imprisonment with hard labour, to which these Acts subject women, are punishments of the most degrading kind.

(5) Because by such a system the path of evil is made more easy to our sons, and to the whole of the youth of England, inasmuch as a moral restraint is withdrawn the moment the State recognises, and provides convenience for, the practice of a vice which it thereby declares to be necessary and venial.

(6) Because these measures are cruel to the women who come under their action—violating the feelings of those whose sense of shame is not wholly lost, and further brutalising even the most abandoned.

(7) Because the disease which these Acts seek to remove has never been removed by any such legislation. The advocates of the system have utterly failed to show, by statistics or otherwise, that these regulations have in any case, after several years' trial, and when applied to one sex only, diminished disease, reclaimed the fallen, or improved the general morality of the country. We have on the contrary the strongest evidence to show that in Paris and other continental cities, where women have long been outraged by this system, the public health and morals are worse than

at home.

(8) Because the conditions of this disease in the first instance are moral not physical. The moral evil, through which the disease makes its way, separates the case entirely from that of the plague, or rather scourges, which have been placed under police control or sanitary care. We hold that we are bound, before rushing into experiments of legalising a revolting vice, to try to deal with the *causes* of the evil, and we dare to believe, that with wiser teaching and more capable legislation, those causes would not be beyond control.'

A friendly member of Parliament wrote:

'Your manifesto has shaken us very badly in the House of Commons; a leading man in the House remarked to me, "We know how to manage any other opposition in the House or in the country, but this is very awkward for us—this revolt of the women. It is quite a new thing; what are we to do with such an opposition as this?" '

The following year Josephine published her first pamphlet on the subject, *An Appeal to the People of England* by 'An English Mother'. In it she stated the arguments against the Acts. Then she pleaded for a more humane way of dealing with the matter of disease: hospitalisation on a voluntary basis, with women doctors. This would be much more likely to decrease the disease than any compulsory scheme. A good moral influence would result in reformed lives as well as cured bodies.

Josephine Butler's crusade against legalised vice and the horrific treatment of women and girls is a record of a woman who relied on God at every step. In 1870 she wrote:

'Thank God all doubt is gone! I can never forget Charles Birrell's prophetic words' (Birrell was a cousin and a Baptist minister) 'sending us forth on our work with confidence . . . Then my husband's benediction! . . . God sent them both to us to dispel all lingering doubts or hesitation . . . We are rebels and for God's holy laws. "What have I to do with peace" any more?'

She had travelled a total of 3,700 miles before the middle of June when she addressed the North of England Council as President. She informed the meeting of her intention to resign her office as soon as possible. She was not to escape from it for three years; but in her speech at this great gathering she made it clear where her priorities now lay:

'It is not because I am not deeply interested in the cause which the Council represents. I am more deeply interested for I see in the education of women one of the most necessary means of freeing poorer women from the awful slavery of which I have seen so much lately . . . Looking back over the year it appears to me as if God in His goodness had said to me, "I approve your motive and your work (education) but you are trying to lay on the topstone while there is an earthquake shaking your foundations. You must first descend to the lowest depths before you can safely build up." And then He showed us a plague spot. He showed us a deadly poison working through the wholesale, systematic, and now legalised, degradation of women. He showed us the ready elements for the speedy overthrow of society, which the *educated* would not be able to stem. Not that our work in the cause of education has in any sense been a failure—far from it, but we need a still larger infusion into these noble schemes for educating the masses in the spirit of self sacrifice, even of martyrdom . . . While therefore I continue to regard the cause of education as a most sacred cause, I come to the present meeting with a sad heart; and *I only propose to relinquish the office I now hold because I feel that God has called me to a more painful one. This work I think is mine* . . . I wish to leave this work in abler hands.'

JOSEPHINE BUTLER—THE FORGOTTEN SAINT

Josephine herself was 'called to deal with the most miserable, to walk side by side, hand in hand with the outcast, the victim of our social sins, whose name one scarcely dares to name in refined society'.

Chapter 3

BY 1870 the Repeal movement was already strong enough to become an electoral issue. A by-election in Colchester gave the National Association for Repeal the first opportunity to directly test its powers. Gladstone's Liberal government was taking no chances. They put up General Sir Henry Storks, a powerful figure who had been Commanding Officer in Malta where he had expressed himself quite satisfied with the administration of the Acts. It was recorded that he regretted only that it was not possible to apply them to the wives of serving men. The Abolitionists' candidate was Dr. Baxter Langley; though nobody seriously expected him to win, it was hoped to cause some embarrassment to the government.

It was thought inadvisable for Josephine to attend the nomination meeting; indeed the men who did so returned in a bad way, having been pelted with stones and filth. Josephine spent her time canvassing among the women of the working class. After an exhausting day, she was about to retire to her room when the landlord of her hotel apologetically had to ask her to leave; a band of men threatened to burn the hotel if she was not at once expelled. A room was secured for her in a respectable working man's house nearby. The change was a great success, and the place was spotless. The next day Josephine held a meeting for women, at which she was not molested. She must have impressed her audience, since she recorded overhearing a woman threatening to kill her husband if he did not vote against the General. Another meeting was not so peaceful. Josephine had to leave by a window, her head swathed in a shawl, and take shelter from a hostile crowd in a disused warehouse. Here she was joined by a local prostitute who got into conversation with her and offered her protection. Guided by the girl, she made her way to a friendly grocer's shop where she hid among the soap and bacon.

General Storks was defeated at Colchester by a margin of 400 votes, a result which gave great encouragement to Josephine and her friends.

One result of the Colchester by-election and the petitions and resolutions now pouring into Westminster was the appointment of a Royal Commission in November 1870. There were twenty-five members, representing both sides of the controversy. It met first in December 1870 and Josephine was called to give evidence on March 18th 1871.

Josephine's own attitude to the Commission may be summed up in her statement after she had replied to their questions:

'Allow me to say I should not be doing my duty to myself, nor to that very large association which I represent throughout the country, if I left your presence without very clearly declaring to you that all of us who are seeking the repeal of these Acts are wholly indifferent to the decision of this Commission . . . We have the word of God in our hands, the Law of God in our consciences. We know that to protect vice in men is not according to the Word of God. We hold that the practical working of an Act, which is vicious in principle, is not a fit subject for an inquiry, and therefore we do not require your verdict any more than if it were to tell us whether there is a God or not. You may be sure that our action in this matter will continue to be exactly the same, even if the Commission pronounces the Acts highly moral. We shall never rest until this system is banished from our shores. I am able to speak with calm confidence, yet with humility, because I believe in the power of prayer. There are tens of thousands throughout this country, men and women, who are daily praying to God that this legislation may be overthrown, the Acts are doomed for this country and for the colonies. This legislation is abhorred by the country as a tyranny of the upper classes against the lower classes, as an injustice practised by men on women, and as an insult to the moral sense of the people. It is this stern resolution which I speak of, which must be fairly faced and grappled with by any Government, and by any medical or other clique which shall determine with a high hand, or plot in secret, to maintain and force upon us an iniquity which is abhorred by Christian England.'

Many of her friends and supporters might have considered this scathing indictment unwise. But in Josephine's opinion there could be no compromise over this issue; how could there be?

Twenty-five men of the highest rank and ability made up the Royal Commission. They were free to rake up all they could to discredit Josephine and her cause, and they tried. They were all men, and they did not spare her finer feelings. Asked what she meant by the 'buying and selling of girls', she replied with complete frankness, 'I have seen girls bought and sold just as young girls were in the slave trade . . . are you not aware that there are gentlemen among the higher classes who will pay so much? When a gentleman sends to a professional brothel for a girl he pays for her. Is that not buying?'

The age of consent was twelve years, and this made possible the sale of mere children into prostitution; a lucrative business was indeed carried on. Josephine had hoped, not for a Royal Commission, but for Parliament to right the wrong. Instead of which it took another fifteen years before the repeal took place, with all the tricks possible used to keep the Acts alive.

E. Moberly Bell, in her biography *Josephine Butler*, gives an account of the interrogation of Josephine by the Commission:

'She spoke of the necessity of "letting in a floodlight on

your doings". She was asked what she meant by *"your* doings". Was it the members of the Commission she was referring to, or the whole of the male population? Unflustered, Josephine replied: "No, I mean the immorality which exists among gentlemen of the upper classes. I will give an illustration of it if you like." It was the last thing the questioners wanted, and the matter was allowed to drop.

'But that was not the end of her questioning. If the Acts were abolished, what could be substituted to achieve the desired ends? Here again, Josephine made her position absolutely clear. No legislation could achieve any satisfactory end, since the only worthy end was the cure—not of the disease, but of the moral corruption which caused it. Certain alterations in the laws were desirable; the laws against solicitation, against procuring and the public flaunting of vice. These laws must apply equally to both sexes, but the work of reclamation, of curing the evil itself rather than the disease which came from it, must be left alone by the State. The work of reclamation could be done only by individuals or by voluntary bodies which must at all costs avoid taking a grant from the Exchequer, since that gave the Government the right to interfere. She spoke a little of her own experience in Liverpool. She was asked tauntingly whether she really believed there were enough individuals to cover the whole country in this work, and she admitted frankly that there were not at the moment, for it asked much of the doer, and not all the privileged were ready to make the necessary sacrifices. But she still believed that interference by the State did more harm than good.

'When one of the Commission asked if she really believed that a fallen woman had any sense of shame left, which should make it possible to redeem her, she expressed surprise at the question. When a young *man* had been known to visit brothels regularly, the question of redemption was never raised, he had merely "sown his wild oats".

It was with this popular opinion that the Commission concurred. In its Report we read: "There is no comparison to be made between prostitutes and the men who consort with them. With the one sex the offence is committed as a matter of gain, with the other it is an irregular indulgence of a natural impulse."

'Josephine had brought letters from her working-class friends in the North, expressing their insuperable hostility to the Acts. These she laid before the Commission, who asked first if they came from genuine working men, and then remarked: "We may as well see them, for no doubt that class takes some little interest in the question." This attitude of superiority to her working-class friends enraged Josephine and she was not sorry to be given the opportunity of saying that she had found a far higher standard of morality among the working classes of the North than among the "Gentlemen" with whom she had discussed the matter. She showed that their opposition to the Acts was due not merely to its power of harming their own daughters, but still more on account of the general degradation of moral standards to which they led. She quoted the words of a Rochdale man: "I should fear the influence of these Acts more for my sons than for my daughters." One working man especially expressed his dread of the power the Acts would put into the hands of an unprincipled foreman, who could utterly destroy the reputation of a girl who worked under him, by false accusations. At once those who resented Josephine's attacks on the upper classes leaped at her. Here was a chance of exposing the inconsistency of this intolerable woman. If the working classes were as moral as she had suggested, what danger could there be in giving them power? Her answer came carefully: "Because the influence of the Act on the population generally is so subtle and powerful that slowly, in the course of years, the moral standard of these men whom I love and admire, will be lowered, and they will be capable of those villainies which they are not now capable of; when I hear that no mistake can be committed by a policeman under these Acts, I am led to contrast that boastful, confident expression with the deep humility of these men, who say 'God knows, if such a power was in my hands, I could not say I might not, in an evil moment, use it.' They are very much more humble. They do not say they could not make a mistake; but these policemen, I believe, contend that they never can err." Some of those sympathetic to Josephine gave her an opportunity to state her fundamental position perfectly clearly: "The elevation of impure and unlawful intercourse, to the dignity of a recognised traffic under legal regulations exercises a most baneful influence on the community."'

On April 4th 1871 Josephine was among those who took to the House of Commons a petition against the Acts containing the signature of 250,283 women. Mr Cowper-Temple, MP, and other members of the Royal Commission were there.

Speaking of her appearance before the Commission, Mr Cowper-Temple remarked, 'No doubt it was a nervous thing for you.' Josephine's spirited reply was characteristic: 'Not at all, sir, but my soul was deeply troubled at the sight of so many men with so base a moral standard as you seem to have and such utter scepticism about God and human nature.' Commented Josephine in a letter to a friend, 'He bit at his lips and looked at his boots and said, "Ah, I fear it is true."'

Of the events of this time, Josephine wrote:

'In spite of great encouragements now and again we were from year to year forced to confess that the prospect of victory was much more distant than we at first imagined. Looking back over those years we can now see the wisdom of God in allowing us to wait so long for the victory. For the mere legislative reform, or rather undoing and repairing, which was our immediate object, was but a small part of the great and vital movement which it was His design to create and maintain for the purifying of the nations; and if we had obtained a speedy triumph there would not have been that great awakening of conscience which we have witnessed, resulting in practical and lasting reforms. At times the struggle between opposing principles was very severe; and hostile criticisms, censures—public and private—accusations, invective, and bitter words fell upon us at certain crises as thickly as the darts of Apollyon on Christian's armour at the entrance of the dark valley. Motives of the worst kind were sometimes imputed, among the most frequent being that of a lurking sympathy, not with the sinners alone, but with their most hateful sins. A certain class of our enemies thought themselves happy, it seemed, in inventing a dart which they believed would strike home in our own case; they sought diligently to spread an impression that some tragic unhappiness in our married life was the impelling force which had driven me from my home to this work, and coarse abuse was varied by hypocritical expressions of pity and sympathy.'

It is strange how history constantly reveals the commonest failing of humanity throughout the ages. So much of our time is taken up in scandal. Where there is none, it is created. Far from recognising in George Butler the character of an outstanding husband, his contemporaries saw him as a weakling who was unable to keep his wife in her place. As for Josephine, there must clearly be something wrong with her married life for her to neglect her home and family to involve herself in matters which should be no concern of a lady. Yet in the face of all this criticism, Josephine continued to feel the secure hand of God. In the inspiration of the Holy Spirit she was able to face the combined opposition of peers of the realm, bishops, Members of Parliament, lawyers, doctors and professional military men. A normal person might just have brazened it out, but Josephine was not brazen.

It is good to relate that even those who opposed her on the Commission recognised her sincerity and courage. There were solid gains, too, in the conversion of two or three members who had previously been prominent supporters of the Acts. The Rev. F. D. Maurice, who on the advice of medical men had actually signed a petition in favour of the Acts, became convinced of his error and published a full retraction; and Mr Charles Buxton MP, who had been a Vice-President of the association in favour of the Acts, resigned this position, acknowledging that 'the Acts have been an utter failure'.

Josephine wrote later, in her biography of her husband:

'In March 1871 I was called to give evidence before the Royal Commission which had been appointed. I was not fully aware until recently, when looking over his letters, how his tender solicitude for me had followed me in all my endeavours; in every varying circumstance. His duties at the Liverpool College forbade him accompanying me to London on this occasion, and even if this had not been the case, he would not have been allowed to remain with me during the examination in the House of Lords. He had unknown to me written to the Chairman of the Commission, Mr Massey, commending me to his kindly consideration. For it was a formidable ordeal, being as I was, the only woman present before a large and august assembly of Peers, Bishops, Members of Parliament, representatives of the military and naval services, doctors, and others; my questioners being in a large majority hostile, and the subject serious and difficult. On the morning before I was called, I received a number of letters, addresses of sympathy, and notices of united prayer for my support from associations of working men of Edinburgh, Glasgow, Newcastle, Leeds, Birmingham and many other towns.'

In a letter to her husband after the Commission she wrote:

'It is over! It was even a severer ordeal than I expected. It was distressing to me, owing to the hard, harsh view which some of these men take of poor women, and of the lives of the poor generally. They had in their hands and on the table everything I have ever written on the subject, and reports of all my addresses, marked and turned down; and some of the Commissioners had carefully selected bits which they thought would damage me in examination. Frederick Maurice was not present, I am sorry to say; but Mr Rylands, Mr Mundella, and above all Sir Walter James, I felt, were my friends. The rest were certainly not so. To compare a very small person with a great one, I felt rather like Paul before Nero, very weak and lonely. But there was One who stood by me. I almost felt as if I heard Christ's voice bidding me not to fear. I handed to the Chairman a large packet of the letters and resolutions from working-men. He said, "We may as well see them; for no doubt that class takes some little interest in the question." I should think so! Let them wait till election times, and they will see! One of the Commissioners asked, "Are these bonâ-fide working-men?" I replied, "Yes, and well-known men. There is more virtue in the country than you gentlemen in high life imagine." He then asked, "If these laws were put in operation in the north, do you believe they would be forcibly resisted?" I replied, "I do." '

Mr Massey, the Chairman of the Commission, wrote to George Butler:

'Reverend and dear Sir, I hope Mrs Butler has not suffered from the long examination which she underwent with so much spirit and firmness on Saturday. I did what I could to shorten the proceedings, but the interest felt in her statements, and the prominent part she had taken in connection with the question led to her detention before the Commission for a too lengthened period.'

Josephine wrote to George:

'I shall be so glad to get back to you, and to breathe

fresher air. I am sure your prayers have been heard in regard to my evidence before the Commission. I don't think I did justice to the Commissioners in my first letter to you. I was so tired and depressed and dissatisfied with myself after the long ordeal, that I saw it all through rather a dark medium. But now I am full of thankfulness to God. I think I may quote to you what Mr Rylands said today to Mr Duncan McLaren and others: "I am not accustomed to religious phraseology, but I cannot give you any idea of the effect produced except by saying that the influence of the Spirit of God was there. Mrs Butler's words and manner were not what the Commission expected; and now some of them begin to take a new view of what they have hitherto called the 'religious prejudice'." He added that Lord Hardwicke came to speak to him afterwards, and that he seemed moved, and said, "If this is a specimen of the strength of conviction in the country on moral questions, we must reconsider our ways." I tell you all this, dear husband, that we may learn more and more to wait upon God, who hears prayer. I spent yesterday with dear Fanny in her rooms. Home tomorrow.'

Lord Mount-Temple, who as Mr Cowper-Temple was a member of the Commission, wrote to Josephine after it had closed its labours and sent out its report:

'I drew up the reasons of the dissent from the report of the majority of the Commissioners and was much pleased to have the concurrence of those who joined with me in signing it. I think you may now be less anxious, though you will not cease from your labours. I believe firmly what you said of a crisis of choice coming to English people. The kingdom of love and purity and righteousness is coming with a new power upon the earth, and the manifestation of it depends upon hearts being ready to receive it. There are some who are looking with faith and hope to the dawn of the coming day; but where are those whose spiritual eyes are opened to perceive how the principles of self surrender and burden-bearing for others can be applied to the new circumstances in which we are living? When Christianity can be extended beyond the sphere of individuals and be thoroughly acted out by numbers of persons in co-operation and in concert, it will produce results never yet seen.'

Josephine's appearance before the Royal Commission can be seen as her finest hour. Her witness on that occasion was undoubtedly her severest test. Up till now, she had provided the leadership and guidance for the movement against the Acts. It was she who had led the attack, she who had been the chief speaker on platforms throughout the land. Always she drew her strength from God, sustained by faith in her mission.

Now for a while she had left her active role. Now she was subjected to fierce questions from the most highly qualified men, specially chosen for the task, most of them convinced of the rightness of the Contagious Diseases Acts, most of them firmly opposed to Repeal, and to all that Josephine's campaign stood for.

Now she was literally standing on her own feet. Every word she had ever spoken in her many public speeches was subjected to the most searching scrutiny; every journey she had taken in the cause of opposition to the Acts open to question. In the witness box, her words were limited to providing the information desired by her inquisitors, information which they drained from her in the most subtle, probing manner. Subjected to sneering and sarcasm about the humble status of many of her followers and supporters, conscious of being a lone woman faced by this formidable panel of men, Josephine kept her dignity, upheld by her faith and absolute assurance in God and in the rightness of her cause.

Millicent Fawcett and E. M. Turner wrote in their book for the Josephine Butler Centenary in 1928:

'It was soon perceived that the Commissioners were deeply

impressed by [her evidence] and especially by the contrast her whole demeanour and attitude of mind afforded to those of some of the promoters of the Acts. She gave an example of endeavouring to accept in all its bearings the teaching given by the Founder of Christianity on the equality of the sexes.'

They relate how she quoted our Lord's words to the woman taken in adultery, 'Neither do I condemn thee, go and sin no more,' and add:

'Again while giving evidence Mrs Butler said in reply to questions that for fifteen years she had devoted her leisure to these unhappy women; she had had five of them living in her house at one time, not as servants but as friends and patients. She had sought them in brothels night and day, in their homes and in the streets, in the workhouses and in Lock Hospitals. . . .

'The industrial question, she urged, emphatically, was all important. "Economics," she argued, "lie at the very root of practical morality." Asked whether women were willing to receive advice as to leading better lives, she replied, "the fallen women are always open to sympathy and influence of those gifted by Providence with the art of reaching hearts." '

Asked to give a general idea as to the means by which the state might check profligacy, Josephine replied that seduction might be punishable by law; that legislation should deal equally with men and women and that bastardy laws should be altered, but she urged that the evil could not be reached by legislation alone. 'The law must be aided by moral influences acting upon both men and women. There should be equal laws to check solicitation in the streets by either sex.' She would never be satisfied by amendments in the Acts; nothing would satisfy her but total repeal.

Chapter 4

IN 1872 George Butler obtained permission to read a paper at the annual Church Congress held at Nottingham, on the subject of 'The duty of the Church of England in Moral Questions'. It was a crowded meeting. As soon as he mentioned the Contagious Diseases Acts, he was howled down. The Bishop of Lincoln, who occupied the chair, was not prepared to act against what was apparently the majority of the meeting, and requested George to abandon his lecture. Very few of the bishops at that time were in sympathy with the cause of Repeal. Clerics may pay lip service to the fact that God moves in a mysterious way, but they were unable to recognise His way in the activities of George and Josephine Butler.

In contrast, there was continued strong support for the cause from the working classes. At a by-election in Pontefract, where the Abolitionists turned out in force to oppose the Government candidate, Josephine and her supporters, making their way to the Town Hall where she was to make a speech, were prepared to go by way of the back alleys. It was the working men who cried out: 'No, never by a back way! Come along through the middle of the crowd and before their windows; we will protect you.' 'Our progress,' recounted Josephine, 'was thus converted into a sort of triumphal procession, Mr Wilson walking first with the Blue Book of the Royal Commission under his arm.'

Josephine gave her own account of an incident during the Pontefract by-election:

'On a certain afternoon when Mr Childers, the Government candidate, was again to address a large meeting from a window of a house, I and my lady friends determined to hold a meeting at the same hour thinking we should be unmolested. We had to go all over the town before we found anyone brave enough to let us a place to meet in. At last we found a large hay loft over an empty room on the outskirts of the town. You could only get to it by means of a sort of ladder leading through a trap door. It soon filled. Stuart had run on to pay for the room in his own name and looked in to see that all was well. The floor was strewn with cayenne pepper to make it impossible to speak. With help he took buckets of water and cleared a good deal. We began our meeting with prayer and the women were listening when smoke appeared through the floor, bundles of straw had been set on fire. Looking down the trap door entrance we saw head after head appear, man after man came in, until they crowded the place. There was no possible exit for us. We were like a flock of sheep surrounded by wolves in one end of the room. They were led by three gentlemen(?), one of them became a candidate for Parliament. Mrs Wilson and I stood in front of the women. She whispered in my ear, "Now is the time to trust in God; don't let us fear." And a wonderful sense of the Divine presence came to us both. You understand, it was not so much personal violence that we feared as what would have been to any of us worse than death; for the indecencies of the men, their gestures and threats, were what I would prefer not to describe. Their language was hideous. They shook their fists in our faces. This continued for some time and we had no defence or means of escape. Their chief rage was directed against me; half a dozen fists were in my face at one time. They filled their vile talk with allusions to the visits under the Contagious Diseases Acts with which they all seemed familiar. It was very clear that they understood that "Their craft was in danger". The new teaching and the revolt of women had stirred up the very depths of hell. We said nothing, for our voices could not have been heard. We simply stood shoulder to shoulder—Mrs Wilson and I—and waited and endured. But it seemed all the time as if some strong angel were present, for when these men's hands were literally upon us, they seemed held back by some unseen power. There was a young Yorkshire woman, strong and stalwart, with bare arms, and a shawl over her head among our flock behind us. She dashed forward and fought her way through the crowd of men, and escaped down the ladder, and running as hard as she could, she found Mr Stuart on the outskirts of Mr Childers' meeting; she said to him, "Come, run! they are killing Mrs Butler." He did run and came up the ladder stairs into the midst of the crowd. As soon as they realised he was our defender they were down on him. A strong man seized him in his arms, another opened the window and they were going to throw him headlong out. I ran forward between him and the window. This was enough to give him time to slip cleverly from between the man's arms on to the floor and glide away to the side where we were. He then asked to be allowed to say a few words to them and with good temper and coolness, he argued that he had taken the room, that it was his, and if they would kindly let the ladies go, he would hear what they had to say. A fierce argument began. Meanwhile stones were thrown into the windows and broken glass flew across the room. While all this was going on hope came at last in the shape of two or three helmeted policemen whose heads appeared one by one up through the trap door. Now we thought we were safe! But no! These Metropolitans had been hired by the Government, and they simply looked at the scene for a few moments with a cynical smile, and left the place without an attempt to defend us. My heart grew sick as I saw them disappear. It seemed now to become desperate.

'Mrs Wilson and I whispered to each other in the midst of the din: "Let us ask God to help us, and make a rush for the entrance." Two or three Yorkshire working-women put themselves in the front and we pushed our way, I don't know how, to the stairs. It was only myself and two or three other ladies that they wanted to do violence to; so if we could get away, the rest would be all right. I made a dash forward and took one flying leap from the trap door to the ground floor below. It was a long jump, but, being light, I came down all right. I was not a bit too soon, for the feet of the men were ready to kick my head as it disappeared down the hole. I found Mrs Wilson after me very soon in the street. Once in the street, of course, these cowards did not dare to offer us the same violence. We went straight to our own hotel, and there we had a magnificent women's meeting.'

Thus once again Josephine demonstrated her utter dependence on God and the power of prayer. Faced by the roughest sort of opposition, including threats to her person, she was able to protect her followers and remain calm even when refused police protection.

How was it possible that Parliament could hold up its head at this time? How could the House of Lords, and the Church, show so little understanding? In 1871 the Royal Commission had positively affirmed the existence of the practice of selling young children for 'infamous purposes' in London and other large towns. Yet it was another fourteen years before Parliament was to act, and then only as a consequence of W. T. Stead's famous 'trumpet blast' in the *Pall Mall Gazette*. Nearly all the authorities in Church and State, law and medicine were adamantly opposed to repeal of the Acts. Yet Josephine was able to say, 'If we could read the present as our successors will read it hereafter, we would thank God that we were born at such a time, and called to put our hands to a work which brings into exercise all the noblest qualities of the human mind and soul.'

If Josephine drew her strength from the reality of her faith in God, she was sustained in it by the support of the poorest and humblest in the land. She records:

'When a very poor woman came to me with a single soiled

petition sheet to be sent to the House of Commons, and I looked at the badly-written names which filled it, and heard her say: "We held a little prayer meeting, Ma'am, and all the women present signed it, well knowing the meaning and with all their hearts"—and when I read a heart stirring memorial to a public man, penned by the trembling hand of a patient in hospital, fast bound by bodily infirmity, but broad in views and high in aims—I felt that an impulse had been given to the cause we have at heart, greater than is given by many an elegant address, or scathing pamphlet by some famous man.'

When, in the winter of 1872, Mr Gladstone paid a visit to Liverpool College, it seemed to many of Josephine's friends a great opportunity for her to speak to him about the women's crusade. Always graciously sensitive to the feelings of others, she declined to embarrass her eminent guest by raising the subject, a point which Gladstone appreciated. He would in any case have had to decline to discuss the matter.

By this time the Government was alarmed enough by the scale of the opposition to try to meet the Repealers with a compromise, yielding certain points of the Acts. It may in fact have been deliberately put forward with the intention of dividing the ranks of the women, and in this it to some extent succeeded. Known as 'Bruce's Bill', after the then Home Secretary, it provided for raising the age of consent from twelve to fourteen, and for 'the harbouring or placing under restraint of any girl under the age of sixteen for purposes of prostitution to be made a misdemeanour.' However the main principles of the Acts remained unchanged. It would still be possible for an innocent girl to be summarily arrested and subjected to degrading examination. More, it would extend the principle to the whole country instead of only thirteen towns. While prostitutes suffering from contagious diseases were to be confined in certified hospitals or prison infirmaries, they could be immediately discharged if they stated their intentions of giving up prostitution. Josephine saw this as meaning that prostitutes were to be cured, not for their own sake, but to protect the 'wicked and immoral men' who would continue to use them. Whereas a girl who sincerely desired to give up the life would, by being discharged from hospital, be deprived of such medical care as was offered.

How could she agree with a Bill telling men, as Bruce's Bill did in effect:

'I can only say to you—immoral men—with whose bodily health I charge myself, that I shall do my best to continue to stand between you and the disease which your vicious actions lay you open to, by falling back upon already existing legal machinery, which I shall make more stringent in its actions upon women of the poorer classes. I shall be able to offer you at the doors of prison infirmaries and certified hospitals, a supply of women who, though not possessing certificates, you may rely on as having passed through the surgeons' hands, and having been made safe for your use. So careful am I that no woman, except such as are made thus safe, shall escape from the aforesaid hospitals and infirmaries, that I have adjudged heavy penalties —arrest without warrant, and imprisonment with hard labour—to any woman who shall attempt to escape. Prison is now the portal to our new system; but there will be no great difficulty in securing that this portal will be made very wide, and that a vast number of women of the poorer classes shall pass through this portal, inasmuch as every penalty shall be enforced with double stringency against all such offences as loitering, begging, "being in any place for the purpose of prostitution (in the opinion of a policeman)" etc. It is, moreover, open to me to create a host of new offences, such as those which have been created in Paris, in order to bring women into the hands of the surgeons.'

In such scathing language Josephine summed up the Bill in a letter to the Liverpool branch of the Repeal Association. An

Act which met the problem only half way was an abomination to her, nothing more than a compromise with evil. 'She was prepared to risk all that had been won, estrange many of her supporters, and break up her party rather than accept Bruce's Bill.'

She wrote:

'A meeting was held in London to consider this bill. There were several delegates of our league from all parts of the country. A long discussion took place, several members of Parliament spoke and it was at last agreed that there was so much good in the Bill that it ought to be accepted by us as an instalment upon which they hoped would follow something more thorough. The question was put to the meeting, and a resolution was voted, apparently unanimously, that the bill should be accepted. I heard a whisper behind me and looking round I saw two pale women (two of my earliest fellow workers) who had not held up their hands (even as I had not) in favour of the acceptance of this measure. I went near them and we whispered to each other that such acceptance would be the ruin of our cause and we asked each other: "What shall we do?" One of the group then stood up and said there were three women there who objected. The President of the meeting, the late Professor Francis Newman, a man who had a profound respect for womanhood, gave a deep sigh, almost a groan, and said: "Gentlemen we must pause! If only one intelligent woman should object to the acceptance of this Bill we must reconsider the whole matter and hear what she has to say!" This note produced a feeling of consternation in the meeting. Two men, however, our most faithful adherents, came at once to our side. The meeting ended in confusion, but almost all that were present had virtually accepted the Government project. There followed many weeks of sad feeling of isolation, and separation from the great bulk of our former adherents; but during those weeks a few of us were silently working and bringing to bear upon the various clauses the principles of British Constitutional Law. We read, we studied, we thought, we prayed, as it were, for our very lives. We published our papers and our books and disseminated them.'

The result was that the Government withdrew the Bill, and to quote Josephine again:

'In course of time the truth prevailed, and almost to a man all those that had wavered came forward, and were more firmly established than before in the principles of our cause; but this result did not come about at once, but slowly one by one, or in small groups. And so we learned hope for the erring, and patience under delays and disappointments.'

This was a severe test for the Repeal movement; but it was ultimately the source of new strength. The movement came out of the ordeal strong, firm, united, determined never again to compromise until the victory was won. For the next fourteen years it settled down to hard dogged work, in Parliament and in the country.

The kind of evil the Repeal movement was fighting to abolish can be shown in all its horror by the story of Mrs Percy, a widow who was harassed by the police until in despair she drowned herself on March 30th 1875. Before taking her life, Mrs Percy had written to the *Daily Telegraph* telling her story: how her husband had been for years confined to bed by illness, until he eventually died, and how she and her daughter Jane, not quite sixteen at the time of her suicide, had supported him and two smaller children by singing at evening parties and taking part in private theatricals at Aldershot. Accused by the police of engaging in prostitution, she was constantly hounded and pressed to sign the dreaded form submitting herself to regular medical examination. In vain she protested her innocence. At length, unable to stand it any longer, she put an end to her life. The child Jane was taken in the Butlers' home, where George was able gently to draw from her the whole story. Later he read it out, just as she had told it, at a protest meeting.

Presiding at the meeting was Mr Edward Backhouse, a rich banker and a member of the Society of Friends, who had once written to George: 'I am glad that the clergy of the Church of England are sending so many signatures to your memorial; but I am sorry the Archbishop of Canterbury had not the courage to present it to the Premier.'

George told the meeting:

'The statement I am about to read to you was drawn from little Jane Percy in the confidence of a quiet Sunday chat after she had been a fortnight in our house and it was written down immediately. We asked her to tell us exactly all she could recollect. She replied: "I will tell you exactly what I saw and remember." And then, speaking for the first time of the bitter trial to which she had been subjected, she said: "They called the police, and ordered my mother to go up to the Metropolitan Police Office and bring me with her. Mamma and I went. We saw there Inspector G——. He was in his room and Mamma was first called in alone. I cannot therefore tell you what happened between Mamma and the Inspector because I was not there. I can only tell you this, that Mamma was never the same person again after that hour. She told me that she assured Inspector G—— that she would rather sign her death-warrant than the paper he gave her to sign. I was then called in. I shall never forget the moment when I stood before Inspector G—— and he accused me. He said: 'Do you know, girl, why you are here?' I replied: 'No, sir, I do not.' He said: 'You are here because you are no better than you should be. You know what that means, I suppose?' I said: 'No, sir, I do not.' He laughed in a horrible way when I said this. I continued to deny that I knew what he meant; for indeed I did not. I knew what a bad character was: there are plenty in Aldershot; but I could not understand that he meant to accuse me and my Mamma of being bad characters. He asked me if we had a 'pass' into the camp. I answered: 'Yes, we have always had one; for we had engagements to sing while papa was lying ill.' He then shouted to someone: 'See that these two women have their passes taken away from them, we will put a stop to all that!' You see, Mamma could not earn a living after this! Mamma said to me as we came out: 'Jenny, this will be the death of me.' She never looked cheerful any more. She was watched by the police wherever she went. Then she wrote that last letter to the *Daily Telegraph*. Soon after that we went away to try to get an engagement elsewhere but could not succeed. Mamma was always crying, and we began to feel what a loss Father was. For, although not able to earn a penny for two years, he was a good friend. We told him of every trouble and he would talk it over and advise us kindly. Nobody but myself knows what Mamma suffered. She could never rest at night; for she said Inspector G——'s face was ever before her as she saw it when he accused her. If she fell asleep she would wake up sobbing and in a fright. I consider that man has been the death of my Mamma. He had said to her at the end: 'I will not leave you alone.' Well, a friend came and asked us to go back to Aldershot. We went back there. Friends used to say to her: 'Cheer up. You will be all the more respected when this is cleared up and the truth is known.' She again said she would choose death rather than do what Inspector G—— wished her to do. He wished her to sign as a prostitute.". . . This ends the girl's evidence; its substance may be regarded as an illustration of the results of this legislation.'

Jane Percy continued to live with the Butlers until they found her a good situation. In her actions as well as in her speech, Josephine was a truly godly woman. She saw the flaw in Bruce's Bill and it cost her many friends. Yet she cared more for the people who would suffer most as a result of its becoming law

Chapter 5

THE Repeal movement grew daily, and its support did not come from working men alone. Abolition Associations were springing up in many towns, among them South Shields, Newcastle, Nottingham, Sunderland, Liverpool and Belfast. In Birmingham, the Mayor and Corporation were in favour of Repeal, and the Mayor chaired a large meeting in support of the cause. Later, another meeting was arranged for women, to be addressed by Josephine.

Two ladies from Bristol, members of the Society of Friends, have left us a description of Josephine at this time. They had come to the meeting expressly to discover what sort of woman she was, 'if she was really one we could follow fearlessly along the dark path.' They were later to be among her closest friends. They wrote: 'The door opened, Mrs Butler came in, slight, graceful, almost young and very beautiful. As she moved to the table she raised her eyes, weighed down with a look of infinite sadness, as if the world's sin and sorrow rested on her innocent head. Surely here was a Christ sent to save us from despair, was the involuntary thought that came into my heart.'

It is as a 'Christ' that I, too, see Josephine, and that is how I want to show her to our confused country today.

Another person to join the cause at about this time was Henry Wilson, the wealthy owner of a smelting works in Sheffield. Like Josephine, he came from a family tradition of bitter hostility to the slave trade. And again like her, he felt called to fight against this new form of slavery. He shared, too, the Butlers' advanced views on marriage, treating his wife as an equal companion and partner in all aspects of their life.

How wise Josephine was to persuade Henry Wilson to lend his business prowess to the crusade. It was her own gift to inspire, fire and encourage. She admitted freely that 'I can never see my way clearly in a great campaign', yet she was the 'way' and the 'life' of the work and, bless her memory, she lent herself wholly to the spirit of God. It was fitting that she should entrust the organising and the slender money bags to the Wilsons.

The forthcoming General Election now occupied Josephine's mind. Abolitionist agents must be appointed to test out candidates and to oppose the enemy of Repeal.

It has been said that Josephine was not easy to please. Of one agent whom she could not bear to have on a platform with her she wrote: 'His manners are against him. He is a vulgar man, in dress, walk and Cockney accent.' She had gone far enough, for she went on, 'I like vulgar people when they are not vulgar in heart like so many of the aristocracy. Yes, I like them. I am so sick of the refined "better" classes, my sympathies are so wholly with the non-privileged even when they drop every "h".'

But all this was secondary to Josephine's main work, of kindling the hearts and minds of her hearers to 'burn up the evil system' of the Contagious Diseases Acts. No one could equal her gift of speaking and carrying her audience with her. She set them on fire. There is no explanation of this other than that she was in constant and personal touch with God. She was possessed with divine power, through her ability to let God into her life. Physically, she was not strong. It was the Spirit of God that drove her. It was the Spirit of God that gave her rest. By her submission to Him, she was contained by Him. It is hard to see a flaw in her, and the hints of weakness and faults suggested by her biographers lack substance in nearly every case because the writers were not on her wavelength. We have seen how her opponents in high places and on the Royal Commission failed to recognise the divine nature of her call—yet the common people saw it. Her husband George saw it. God and she were in tune, and

JOSEPHINE BUTLER—THE FORGOTTEN SAINT

George sealed it with his co-operation and blessing.

Again, there cannot have been many occasions when the leader of a movement has dissented from the opinions of the vast majority of the members, knowingly risking the entire break-up of the movement, yet prepared to face even this calamity, knowing that she was right. A great number of educated, thinking women were taken in by Bruce's Bill, and convinced that it was a fair and generous compromise. There are writers who have felt that Josephine was wrong to oppose the Bill. She was not; and the proof is that her strong attitude of 'no compromise' towards Bruce and the Acts eventually brought victory. Josephine saw clearly that Bruce's cold and unbending attitude to the recommendations of the Royal Commission meant that he was not to be trusted. She had spiritual insight, and the strength of character to obey it.

Josephine was tough enough to take physical violence and refuse to be deterred by it. At a meeting in Glasgow, 200 medical students broke up her meeting, refusing to listen to her. From there she travelled on to Leeds, Bristol, Plymouth and Woolwich. At a town in South Wales, it is said, she concluded her speech by quoting with great effect a denunciatory passage from the book of Isaiah. A reporter who was present referred to this as 'a tirade of language which, coming from the lips of a lady, we would rather not reproduce!' In 1872 she travelled 3,700 miles and addressed 99 meetings and four conferences. It says much for her powers of endurance that, because of lack of funds, all her travel was in third class railway carriages.

Josephine had to educate her supporters, who were rightly shocked by the Acts and by the treatment of women, but largely ignorant of the wider social problems which lay behind these measures. In reply to those who called for new laws to replace the Acts, she was adamant:

> 'My motto is no legislation at all on prostitution, for all such legislation will press on women only. But even if it did not, I have no faith in it. For our legislative programme I

would ask *only repeal*. No alternative, no substituted alternative; but let it be understood clearly that our "social" programme is not the same. As private or associated workers, societies, etc., we are bound to do all we can to attack and heal the miseries of society, and to reclaim the fallen, and prevent immorality. The very fact of leaving the State to do it by its laws will lessen the sense of personal responsibility and weaken the fervour of charity in all, the best of us, so that our hands will hang down and we shall leave it to the State to do this deep, difficult, holy work.'

At a conference she reminded her hearers:

'We are not met to discuss principles; there is a call to battle, and for that we have to get our guns and earthworks ready, there is no time for mere talk . . . we are here to plan "work" and not "jaw".'

Josephine was a general leading her troops into battle for the absolute and entire repeal of the Contagious Diseases Acts; with all that followed from them, for mere children came within the scope of the Acts since a man was legally allowed to use a child of twelve, if he could claim that she had given her consent. For Josephine, the Holy War was on.

Hopes were pinned to the General Election to bring about repeal. The result was depressing for the Abolitionists, who had hoped that 'Irish Land Bills and the like will not hereafter be the engrossing matters for Parliament to deal with'. The fact was that the Conservatives won and were convinced that the system of regulation and official brothels must continue. A medical congress held in Vienna passed a resolution expressing the conviction that regulation was the only possible way of controlling venereal diseases and called for every port in Europe to adopt the measures and enforce regulation.

A very different tone prevailed at a meeting of the Ladies National Association; they were still determined to do what they could to bring about repeal, but they were downcast.

Josephine urged that they must continue to pray. If their prayers up to now had not been answered in the way they had hoped, then God must have some even greater purpose; and His time had not yet come:

> 'I think it is better for this country and for the world that this struggle should be prolonged and should become hotter—until this seven times heated fire has more completely separated the dross and the gold, and purified the moral atmosphere. This conflict is not for England alone. The eyes of Europe are upon us, and the spirit manifested among us is full of significance to many who have long mourned on this evil in other countries. The longer and more earnest our struggle is, the more effectually will it loosen the chains of wickedness in other parts of the world.'

Josephine's personal conviction that God was in control was born of a deep personal prayer life. Her patience throughout the whole campaign, and the strength of her belief that God was at work despite appearances, are little short of miraculous. Year after year Bills were drafted and successfully piloted through the Lords, but session after session they were destroyed by the House of Commons. The most urgent reform recommended by the Royal Commission, that of raising the age of consent from twelve, was put aside. If the matter was raised by a member of Parliament, it was met with roars of laughter, as were all matters concerning women and girls. Through all this Josephine displayed a gracious and saintly dignity, and took her followers with her. Only God can know how she was able to carry such a burden. There can be no explanation apart from God-given strength, for flesh and blood alone, however determined, could not have borne it. The attitude of the Government was contemptuous and loathsome. The upper classes, the wives and children of Lords and members of Parliament, were a class apart, entitled to privilege; the poor did not matter.

But 1874 was not to be all black for the Repealers. The defeat of Gladstone's government left the Rt Hon. James Stansfeld, former President of the Local Government Board, without office. He was thus able to devote his whole strength to the repeal of the Contagious Diseases Acts. Hitherto, he had not studied the Acts in detail, assuming that the doctors' opinion must be accepted. Now, in spite of a personal aversion to the subject of prostitution, a study of the Acts convinced him that he must devote himself to the cause.

If certain sections of the Press had totally ignored Josephine and the movement, it could not ignore so great a man as James Stansfeld. *The Times* regretted 'that a statesman of Mr Stansfeld's eminence should identify himself with such an hysterical crusade.' To Josephine, this public alliance of an eminent figure gave fresh strength. W. T. Stead commented:

'It was an odious duty from which all Right Honourables had hitherto shrunk. Right Honourables there were in plenty who voted for and enforced the Acts, from Mr Gladstone downwards. Right Honourables who would risk reputation, position, career for a cause such as this—there was only one, and his name was Stansfeld . . . Mr Stansfeld had however caught from Mazzini, with whom he had lived for many years in closest intimacy, something of that divine thirst for self-sacrifice which enables men, even when they have sat in Cabinets, to give up all and follow the supreme call of Duty and Pity.'

So, in 1874, Stansfeld allowed his name to appear as Vice-President of the National Association for Repeal. His first speech was at a meeting of the Association in Bristol in October. Josephine, who was present, described the occasion. 'It was a striking and pathetic appearance. He had been alone in his room all day and looked pale and nervous when he appeared on the platform. He passed on to me a little note and among other things he wrote: "I am so thankful for the women's prayers."'

An elderly clergyman remarked to Josephine that it was like a confession of faith: 'He seemed to invoke the presence of the Divine Being as he stood with his hands uplifted.' Josephine commented: 'This is true. It was felt to be the utterance of feelings long pent up, and was like a trumpet blast to call us afresh to the battle as well as the keynote of the future —full of courage and confidence.'

Stansfeld knew he was sacrificing his political career when he took that step. His biographers, J. L. and Barbara Hammond, said of him that 'he stepped out of his place as a Radical Leader to join a ship that looked as if it was sinking.'

But it did not sink.

Chapter 6

JOSEPHINE had known from the beginning that the evil against which she was fighting had long existed in other countries of Europe, and she had friends on the Continent who shared her concern. In the winter of 1874 she undertook the first of many visits abroad to encourage international opposition to the threat.

Many of her friends and supporters contemplated her visit with heavy hearts. Josephine herself felt a strong reluctance. The Society of Friends summoned a meeting in Birmingham to wish her God-speed. Josephine wrote, of this occasion: 'As we sat during one of those calm silences which I so much love in Friends meetings, when God seems more present than when any voice of prayer is breaking the hushed stillness, I did not think any more of the cold winter, long journeys, cynical opposition and difficulties I was going to meet.' The text came into her mind: 'Behold I have set before thee an open door, and no man can shut it.'

She set off in December, armed with many letters of introduction. During the Channel crossing she found in a notebook an envelope addressed to 'My Dear Wife—to be used when we are separated from each other.' It contained a prayer:

'Thou, O God, art the God of all families of the earth; on Thee we depend for protection from all dangers, for preservation from all evil. We commend ourselves especially to Thy Fatherly care during our sojourning in foreign lands. Watch, we pray Thee, over every member of our family. When scattered, reunite us. When in trouble, comfort and relieve us. Lead us by the Holy Spirit, and keep us all in faith and hope, in purity and in holiness, and in the exercise of love one towards another . . . enlarge our sympathies with all orders and degrees of men. Dispose those that are high in station and influence to receive us kindly for the sake of Jesus Christ. Give Thy blessing to the efforts that shall be made to reclaim souls from the curse of sin, and from all cruel, immoral, and unjust laws. Bless the labours of all Thy servants for the establishment of the Kingdom of Christ on earth.'

If ever an answer had been needed to the suggestion that all was not well in the marriage between George and Josephine, this prayer was evidence enough.

Josephine spent 'ten days of very arduous work' in Paris. George wrote to her in a letter:

'The weather in Paris seems to be as severe as in England, and I am glad you take a carriage to go about. I am glad also to think you have one of our sons with you. Tell my dear Stanley to be sure to look out for the best works in the Galleries of the Louvre, a list of which I herewith send; and tell him not to do as the Parisians do while in Paris, but to do as he has always done, and so make glad the heart of his father and mother. Be sure you see Lord Lyons, and present Lord Derby's letter to him.'

Her reception from officials was one of cynical opposition. E. Moberly Bell gives an account of her visit to Lecour, the Prefect of Police, in an office designed to exalt his importance:

'. . . its white marble staircase, the guards and uniformed flunkeys in attendance, the gold letters above the door proclaiming the "Service des Moeurs"—in her opinion an outrageous title for an office which should more fitly have been described as designed for the service of "Débauchés". She was shown into the sanctum with impressive ceremony and given a paper to read while Lecour was concluding an interview with an earlier caller. As she sat and listened, behind her paper, the man's arrogance and self-satisfaction became more and more apparent and by the time he was at leisure to attend to her she was blazing with suppressed fury. She rose to her feet, disdaining the proffered chair and looked him fully in the face throughout the interview. We need not be surprised to learn that he appeared to quail before her. When she asked him a question the answer came in a flood of talk, designed to prevent her from saying more. When she asked him if vice in Paris had increased or diminished in the preceding three months, he replied eagerly, without realising that it condemned his own system, that it increased all the time and added hastily that this was due to the "coquetry" of the women. As the interview proceeded he became somewhat flustered and made statements that she was able to refute from one of his own books; whereupon he attempted a diversion by declaring that he was as earnest a Christian as she was, to which Josephine replied that that might be so, but she was there to talk not about Christianity but about justice.'

She did obtain from the Prefecture a permit to visit St Lazare, 'prison, hospital and general depot for those accused only of vagabondage, or who were seeking work and had no friends'. It was only with difficulty that she gained admission. At first she knocked on the door with her hands. Receiving no reply, she nearly gave up. But she remembered the promise of the 'open door'. Picking up a large stone she hammered at the door until someone came. A nun showed her round. In the exercise yard women and girls—some little more than children—walked round in silence. Though they slowed down to stare at her, she was not allowed to talk to them. Of her tour of the rest of the prison she has left no record. It was an experience so horrible and painful she could never bring herself to speak or write of it. In a rare allusion to the experience she said:

'My heart was ready to faint within me as I marked the horrible development and influence of that institution which poor England in her folly had recently adopted. I was watched by the police, and my movements reported. Yet we had much ground for encouragement in the fact that the best men and women in Paris from the first seconded our efforts, although they did not as yet see much hope of the success of our enterprise.'

Glen Petrie, in his book *A Singular Iniquity* gives a terrible account of conditions in St Lazare at this period, based on a contemporary report by Yves Guyot, member of a commission of inquiry into prisons. I cannot pay tribute enough to those who have the gift of words and, like Glen Petrie, pursue their researches into the dark passages, given only a candle and a strong wind to guide them. His keenness and care for historical accuracy urges him on to describe the depths of this awful prison:

'Guyot's first impression of St Lazare was the smell of the yards which were used as a depository for every kind of slop, and the way in which this stench penetrated every room of the buildings to mingle with what he called the "shut-up" smell which was the result of gross over-crowding in the wards. He noticed that the girls' uniform-dresses were filthy, as were the girls themselves. This was hardly surprising, since they were permitted neither to wash their clothes nor their bodies—the nuns insisting that they should never be permitted to undress lest they commit an offence against modesty. The nuns, however, did instruct their charges in the use of a syringe, which, as Guyot pointed out, since it was never washed, probably accounted for the incidence of venereal disease among Paris prostitutes.

'The girls lived and slept in dormitories containing four rows of beds crowded together in such a way as to provide exactly half the space which government regulations laid down regarding ordinary prisons. Their working day began at 4.45 a.m. when they were woken up to cries of *Vive Jésu!* By 5 a.m. they had made their beds, completed the minimal toilet allowed to them and were assembled in the workrooms for the Morning Offering. There, they worked until 8.45 a.m. when they received their first meal of the day, soup consisting of water-broth containing a single carrot or leek. Afterwards they walked in the yard until 9.45 a.m., when they returned to work. At noon they had lunch consisting of bread which had been dipped in vegetable soup (the soup itself being reserved for the staff), after which, they worked again until 3 p.m., when they received their last meal of the day, a plate of beans. They then had an hour of recreation spent in walking silently around the yard, worked until 7 p.m., had Night Prayer and went to bed.

'Any breach in the regulations—failure, for instance to genuflect when a nun passed by—meant removal to the punishment rooms, as did refusal to submit to being placed *en carte*. These rooms consisted of windowless and airless garrets whose sole furniture consisted of one tub for the performance of natural functions, which was rarely emptied. In these garrets, girls spent day and night, fed at irregular intervals on bread and water which they had to consume without the use of their hands, since they were bound in strait-jackets. Guyot inquired of the Mother Superior in charge how long girls were confined under such conditions. They remained there, answered the Mother Superior, until they volunteered to be placed *en carte,* or, in the case of those who had offended against the regulations, until she— the Mother Superior—was satisfied that they were sincerely contrite. There was a second alternative she might have mentioned: until, in the permanent semi-darkness and ammoniac dung-heap stench, they went insane—a condition always put down by the medical officers as being the result of advanced syphilis.

'Finally Guyot visited the wing reserved for children suspected of having been engaged in prostitution. Their dormitory consisted of a darkened room, without window or lights, and their beds were wooden cages. The reason offered for this was that these children must not pick up immodest habits by observing each other as they retired to bed, and the cages ensured against them instructing each other in lesbian practices in the darkness. He asked what happened to such children after they had been released. Lecour, who was with him during this visit, replied that the authorities wrote to the *mairie* of the district where they had been born, and if the officials of the *mairie* could not locate their parents or guardians, they were apprenticed to a licensed brothel.'

This was the horror which Josephine felt too much to put into writing. No wonder girls would commit suicide rather than submit to arrest by the dreaded Police des Moeurs.

Josephine carried with her a letter from Cardinal Manning addressed to all Catholic clergy:

'This lady has undertaken a difficult and a very needful mission. I beg you to give her such assistance and encouragement as you can in her work of charity, and to recommend her to persons who may have any influence in the matter of the reform which she seeks to promote. No Catholic who fears God can refuse to give his allegiance to the sacred cause which she has espoused.'

A French worker for reform, Mme Simon, bore witness to Josephine's personal sanctity at the first conference in Paris:

'I think your mission will not have any success in France because it is too high and holy to be understood here.'

Ten months later the same lady wrote:

'You are not under any illusion, for your voice is indeed at present but a voice in the wilderness; but be of good courage, for those who do not understand you today will understand you tomorrow.'

Josephine wrote to Mr Stansfeld from Paris:

'I should like our friends to know how much the little faithful band of sympathisers in Paris recognise our mission as from God. There has lately been a great religious movement in France as in some parts of England. Meetings of prayer are held constantly. There is a feeling of expectation, discomfort, in the belief that action, aggressive action, ought to follow and must follow, the deepening of spiritual life, and a clearer understanding of their personal relations with the Father in heaven. They have been feeling it is not enough to meet and pray and to try for themselves to draw nearer to God. There must be a deeper meaning to this spiritual awakening; there must soon be a call to battle ... I spoke to them of what I felt, *and that the only reason of our being on earth at all is to be combatants; that the only condition of our spiritual health is war, against the whole kingdom of Satan and against all evil things* ... They saw and confessed that the deepened personal life of the soul meant increased responsibility and they recognised the guidance of God in this second call; and as the path became clearer to me, I saw how "God leads the blind by a way they know not of".'

After ten busy days in Paris, Josephine and Stanley joined the rest of the family for a holiday in the South of France and Italy. She wrote of her relief at being once again alone with her family.

'Eleven hours in a train, wrapped in a large rug, with foot warmers and *no responsibility for eleven hours!* I almost laughed to myself for joy.'

But even on holiday she was unable to keep away from

the problem which dominated her mind. In Italy, state prostitution was flourishing, though it had not been established without opposition. The Pope, Pius IX, had protested, and people were divided on the issue. Josephine at once found friends in Rome. A young politician, Guiseppe Nathan, seems almost to have been converted by her. He met her at a time when he had just lost his English wife, and his friends feared for him. Josephine showed him loving sympathy and helped to take him out of himself. In turn, he introduced her to Deputies who might help her, and secured an interview for her with Cavour, the Minister of Justice and Police. Several meetings were arranged, and plans were laid for an Association to forward the movement.

She had hoped for a complete rest with her sister Hatty in Naples, instead of which the news of her coming had got around and many were eager to hear her speak. By this time the rest of the family had returned to England. Josephine wrote to George:

'We have had an excellent meeting here . . . You know that my one object in coming here was to see my darling Hatty, and to rest awhile with her in her beautiful home. I neither planned nor expected a continuance of my mission here; but God ordered it otherwise, and without our seeking it at all the work *came* to us. Two gentlemen called and gravely desired to learn whether I would address a company of friends on the subject of our mission, if they undertook the arrangements. I said I could not refuse their request. They then asked me to accompany them to the English Consul to ask him to preside at the meeting. We parted at the Consul's door, they to get circulars printed and I to confer with Hatty as to ladies who might support us. In every step, however, the initiative was taken by others and we only followed the guidance which was so distinct that we could have no doubt at all about the Voice saying: "This is the way, walk ye in it". How often have I longed to have Hatty, my childhood's beloved companion, associated with me in this holy work . . . I wish every moment you were here. At the meeting we had no expressed opposition, but I was aware of an opposing current . . . and it was an English doctor . . . he entered with a great bundle of the *Lancet* under his arm. It makes one smile to see that miserable *Lancet* brought forward as an authority in great moral and humanitarian questions like this. You can believe that Hatty and I returned to the house full of thankfulness to God . . . I should tell you that a resolution was passed of sympathy with the work and the workers.'

In a letter thanking her sister, she wrote:

'Going from city to city, tired and weary, always to meet with sharp opposition and cynicism, and ever new proofs of the vast and hideous oppression, is like running one's breast upon knife points, always beginning afresh before the last wound is healed. You understand don't you? I utter this little cry to you, but I am not despondent. This is only physical weakness, I think, for I have to praise God for good work accomplished and for souls inspired to work. "I know that my Redeemer liveth." The hour of our redemption has struck! I say "our" for we have not only "remembered" those in bonds as being bound with them, but actually *"suffered with them"* in spirit for long, long years. This may be but the beginning of the breaking of our bonds, and to our finite minds the *Deliverer* may seem long in coming. To the Lord a thousand years are but as one day . . . ; but the time is coming—is coming most surely. One thing we know, and that is, that all this cruelty and sin, this blinding and misleading of souls, this selfish profligacy, this slaughter of the innocents, the organised vice, this heavy oppression, this materialism which sets the body above the soul, profaning the sacred name of science, and making of her a "procuress to the Lords of Hell"—all this we know is hateful in the eyes of the Holy God and we know that it must *perish* before the light of His countenance, when the arm of the Lord shall be revealed and when His own arm shall bring salvation. Even out of the depths therefore we will praise Him, and rejoice for the day that is coming. Be strong in the faith my dear one; do not despair even for those poor captured victims, from their childhood forced into sin and shame, whose sorrowful sighing seems for a time to rise in vain to heaven. *Can we love them so much and doubt that God loves them far more than we?* Our utmost pity is but a drop compared with the ocean of His pity for them. I feel a kind of triumph in that beautiful arrangement by which He has chosen the weak things of this world to confound the strong. It matters nothing at all what we are, provided we are entirely willing to be made the instruments of His Will, His agents in this world. I do not think we know the meaning of the word *"strength"* until we have fathomed our own utter weakness. I sometimes think of the lines about the "Steadfast Prince" . . .

'Did I tell you how I had been pleasantly haunted before I left home by the words "Behold I have set before thee an open door, and no man can shut it"? I often used to wake up suddenly at night with a fear lest I had been presumptuous to think of such a mission as this; and then these words would again and again sound in my soul, and almost in my ears as if an angel had spoken them. Yes, it is true if *that* hand opens the door, not all the powers of earth nor of hell can prevail to shut it.'

In thus pouring out her soul to her dearest sister, Josephine reveals all the shades of doubt which beset her in the valley of the shadow of death. She shows the many guises of the strength of the enemy, and the beauty and wonder of perfect faith and absolute trust in God. It is the perfect poetry of the humble, self-sacrificing, obedient saint.

She carried people along with the optimism that comes only from complete reliance on God. Returning to Paris, by way of Switzerland where she made further important contacts, notably a M. Aimé Humbert of Neuchâtel, she wrote to Joseph Edmondson:

> 'I want to tell you once more how wonderfully God has worked in this matter. I am filled with awe and gratitude when I think of it. I see His hand in all and I think your prayers have followed and surrounded me.'

Black as things were in Paris, Josephine saw the possibility of help in many areas, and discovered small groups which needed support and help from England. Could the supporters of the movement be content with achieving repeal in England alone? If the situation on the Continent were left unchanged, would England ever be free of infection? Legalised prostitution had come from the Continent, and it would come again. She saw more strongly than ever the need for an international effort to fight this evil thing. She received the full backing she asked for. She was asking very little compared with what she was giving. No leader could give more than she; she was giving all, but braving all.

She wrote a letter to George shortly before leaving Paris in February 1875. It gives a glimpse of her loving concern and complete identification with those who laboured for the same cause.

> 'It was a relief and rest to me after seeing many sad places, to pay a visit to the "Maison des Diaconnesses" and to see the good work done there—the schools, hospitals and refuge. I dined with the Diaconnesses, and afterwards one of them took me to see the poor girls they rescue from misery and vice. They were all assembled and this Diaconnesse said to them in a sweet and gentle voice: "I want you to look at this dear lady, my children. Yes, look at her well, for she is your friend, and perhaps you may never see her again. She is our friend; she has come to Paris to say that our bonds shall be broken." And she continued, speaking almost as a person speaks in a dream,

and very solemnly, "Our bonds shall be broken. A time shall come when vice shall no more be organised and upheld by law, to crush us down to hell. You understand what I mean, my children. Ah, you understand too well! She has come to Paris to oppose the great machinery which makes it so easy to sin, and so hard to escape. She brings you a message from Jesus today, my children, and asks you to love Him and to look forward in hope. For our bonds shall be broken—ours; for we are sisters, we suffer with you." She explained further to them, very delicately and solemnly, till one saw they began to feel they had a part with us in the good war. I said a few words and then we all sang a hymn together, about our bonds being broken, at the end of which this Diaconnesse played a few notes on her harmonium, on which she had accompanied us, in which there came a minor tone of sadness for a moment, which seemed to express the hidden agony of the heart so well known to us, while we spoke only of hope to the poor girls.'

Chapter 7

THAT same year Josephine's health broke down. She returned from her Continental travels looking 'worn with her winter campaign but always graceful and dignified, possessing herself so calmly that no harm can touch her'. She knew that she needed rest and longed for Liverpool and home. But she must not only make a report of her work on the Continent, but while the interest and keenness was alive among the new friends overseas, a link must be established. Josephine was the obvious person to make and keep the contacts. So it was resolved that Miss Tanner should take over the leadership of the Ladies' Association at home, leaving Josephine free to create the British and Continental Federation for the Abolition of Government Regulation of Prostitution. Stansfeld became its President and Josephine and Henry Wilson its joint Secretaries.

Meanwhile Josephine was taking stock of the knowledge she had acquired on her tour. With the help of M. Humbert she set to work with the publishers to compile statistics and facts about legalised prostitution in many countries. Facts must be obtained from a wide area, for they stood as indestructible witnesses of the folly of the attempt to regulate vice.

'How much more powerful, how overwhelming in fact', she wrote to Aimé Humbert, 'would it be for our opponents, and how strengthening for our cause, if we could show facts and statistics gathered from every country, and over a larger period of time.'

So reports were received from Italy, France, Germany and other countries. Josephine recorded:

'On every hand there is confession of the failure of regulation.'—'Mireur, Jeannell, Diday, Deprès, Pallasiano, Huet, Crocq, all confess to hygienic failure.'

Pathetic facts emerged. In another letter to M. Humbert she wrote:

'Four-fifths of the poor girls used are orphans, many are foreigners in the country of their enslavement; many are young widows. Does not our God, who is the God of the fatherless, of the widow and of the stranger, take note of these things? You see that, in a year or two, we shall have a mass of evidence against this system which will give the doctors and materialist legislators a hard task to refute. I care little for men who accuse me of mere sentiment and of carrying my hearers by feeling rather than with facts and logic. Now for the first time they are asked to look upon it as a question of human nature, of equal interest to man and woman; as a question of the heart, the soul, the affections, the whole moral being. As a simple assertion of one woman speaking for tens of thousands of women those two words: *"We rebel"* are very necessary, and very useful for them to hear. The cry of women, crushed under the yoke of legalised vice, is not the cry of a statistician or a medical expert; it is simply a cry of pain, a cry for justice and for a return to God's laws in place of these brutally impure laws invented and imposed by man . . . This is the voice of a woman who has suffered, a voice calling to holy rebellion and to war. It will penetrate. Then by and by we shall come down on our opponents with the heavy artillery of facts and statistics and scientific arguments on every side. We will not spare them, we will show them no mercy. We shall tear to pieces their refuge of lies, and expose the ghastliness of their covenant with death, and their agreement with hell. We and our successors will continue to do this year after year until they have no ground to stand upon.'

A Berne paper, referring to Josephine, commented:

'These English women are remarkable, they unite with their great freedom a dignity seldom seen elsewhere ... We have not dared to associate women with us, as is done in England in this work of moralisation. Mrs Butler, an instrument prepared by God Himself for this combat, brings to us troops of female auxiliaries whom many men will fear to meet and with good reason.'

It was not that English women were so brave, but that one woman responded to the touch of God Himself; Josephine allowed herself to be used and led by God—and she a devoted wife and mother and home-lover. Her leadership and total commitment inspired others to follow. She won men to the fight, too, her latest and most important conquest being M. Humbert, who gave up all other work and put himself entirely at Josephine's disposal.

But Josephine's breakdown was serious and she was ordered by her doctor to rest absolutely. Although the loss of her inspired leadership was grievous, it spread the load and other able people took charge and kept up the morale of the movement. Josephine urged her followers to 'be strong and of good courage and know that the battle is God's'. From April to June she was inactive, but the work did not stand still.

From the beginning the medical profession had stood by the Acts. Now there came a breakthrough. Dr Nevins, on the staff of a teaching hospital in Liverpool, made a thorough investigation into the effectiveness of the Regulations, ignoring all propaganda. The result of his findings was against Regulation. He could find no evidence that it had diminished disease. Dr Nevins founded the National Medical Association (for Abolition) and he started a new journal, *The Medical Inquirer*. The first issue came out in March 1875. It was also at this time that the sad story of the death of Mrs Percy was made public. The *Daily Telegraph* took up the matter and the Regulations were discredited. The National Association also held a meeting of protest at the Westminster Palace Hotel, against this further abuse of power by the police and the Regulations. Harcourt Johnson moved a second reading of his Repeal Bill in June. He was defeated, but the debate was treated seriously and without derision. The principal opponent was the Judge Advocate General, who was however reported as saying of the women: 'I say all honour to them for it, and I should be the last to join in the outcry which has been raised against these who have so devoted themselves.' In this debate, Gladstone, belatedly, voted for Repeal.

Josephine's superhuman ability to cope with organisation and direction as well as delivering numerous speeches in the course of her fight would be enough for the toughest and ablest of men. How she managed to fit into her terrific programme time for reading and writing is beyond understanding apart from divine strength. In 1876 she wrote *The Hour before the Dawn*, an appeal to men. It was translated into French the same year as its publication in England. Josephine's name did not appear on the work until six years later and when the second edition was printed. The book expressed the greatest sympathy with men as well as women. She looked back to the darkness of her own soul when 'anger, fear and dismay filled my heart . . . I could see no God.' She saw sin as the law of the world and Satan as its master. 'Does not God care?' she asked. Here is the battle, the saint taken through the valley of the shadow of death. But she wins through to the cross itself. She pleads to see the Lord's own heart, she asks for knowledge of His attitude towards His lost world. The measure of the depth of her spiritual searching into the heart of God is the secret of her power to suffer and still to go on. She has attained the pain-filled yet liberating spirit of unyielding service to God for man. She cannot compromise with evil; black is black and white is white. Here is the story of the cross with its love of humanity and its giving spirit. Josephine turns to God, and to love as we see it in Christ.

I do not think I have ever known such a loving partnership as that between George and Josephine; the blend would seem to be perfect. Perfect in God. Two most sacred letters she allowed herself to write about their love are what they are because they come out of a deep love and a deep belief in God. Read them! Josephine herself wrote: 'The following letters were not intended for any eye but that of the friend of my childhood; the sister to whom they were addressed.

Berne, August 13th, 1876

'Much business comes upon us now, after our pleasant excursions. I feel rather sleepy and stupefied, so lately down from those blazing snows. George is soon leaving for Liverpool. I am sorry to lose him, the dearest and gentlest of men. One's heart so yearns for him when he is gone. It has answered well my going to him at Zermatt, for it has been such an increase of pleasure to him; and in my heart pangs about his returning home alone I shall have a real consolation in recollecting that our last mountain days were spent together. He asks so little and is so grateful for every good thing. I think he was touched by my jogging quite alone on my horse all the way from Sierre in the Rhône valley to the Riffel, where I saw him sitting on the hillside. He had given up the thought of my coming on account of the storms and damaged roads. He was sketching. I shall never forget his face of joy when he recognised me coming up through the woods. I thought he would have broken his neck, bounding over the rocks to meet me.'

August 14th, 1876

'I got your last welcome letter at breakfast, and left the good Bernerhof tea untasted until I had read it through. I then showed George your kind words about him. His look was tender and pleased when reading it. He never draws any praise on himself, nor seems to expect it; but a little affectionate praise is well bestowed on him, he is so grateful. I feel ridiculously much this parting from him, and every parting from him; ridiculously I mean because it is only, please God, for a short time. But about him I have the yearning of heart which one feels over an infant or an aged person, or some other holy thing which one has let go out of one's care and sight for a time. His presence is like wholesome air. People do not notice it much perhaps, but when it is withdrawn one stretches out one's hands wearily and painfully to try and grasp again that good thing which is gone. I often wish I could describe his character, just as it is, in a poem or a book. Anyone would rise from reading it with a prayer, "May God send us many such men upon the earth." It is so sweet to me that *you* appreciate him, and that your keen, loving insight makes you able to see the loveliness and nobleness of his character which few quite see, and that you can understand me when I speak of the love of which God alone knows the depth and the far-reaching tenderness—a love which grows and deepens with years. Except for the pain it would give to him, I always hope I may die first. For if he were to die and leave me, I do not say I could not live or work any more, but I fear I should fall into a state of chronic heartache and longing which would make me rather useless, and perhaps a weariness to others, who would never fully understand what and who I had lost. I do not often speak of him thus, but this once I cannot help it; your tender appreciation of him makes it impossible for me not to speak . . . Last night we had a lovely sunset. We saw the rose tints on the Eiger and Jungfrau from the balcony, and I thought of you and wished I could fly over to Grindelwald and sit on the bench beside you, and watch it with you.'

I have felt compelled to quote this beautiful tribute of a

wife to her husband. It reveals the saintliness of both. But it also shows the sensitive nature of this woman who was called by God to challenge and defeat legalised prostitution in England and to force the repeal of the Contagious Diseases Acts. It was agony and sweat all the way for Josephine. It was more; it was leaving hearth and home, and separation from the man she adored, and who adored her.

It could have been the attraction of a kindred spirit that led her in 1878 to write a life of Catherine of Siena. Josephine, too, had had visions and heard voices, and she would have had no difficulty in understanding the close communion between God and Catherine. She herself felt the touch of God, and would spontaneously turn to God in praise and petition at any moment. She walked with God, as did Catherine, who was unafraid and never forced herself on the weak and erring Pope. The likeness between the two women was strongest in the element of prayer. Life and death were cheap enough in Catherine's day, and if she had faltered in her faith the cunning doctors in theology would have had her burned; they had brought her from her sick bed to answer their clever questions. Josephine's lone task before the Royal Commission was not quite so dramatic, but had she faltered and become afraid her credit would have gone, for there was little mercy and the devil was busy.

No doubt Josephine found comfort and strength in studying the life of St Catherine. It is strange to find in a Bible-reading Protestant such as Josephine a kinship with the mass-faith, hours-keeping Catherine. But the book is beautifully written and with sympathetic understanding, out of a common love of God—a love which had to find its expression in action.

Chapter 8

THE Federation and links with Europe slowly brought to light the vicious organisation behind Regulation and the cruelties to women and girls involved in the system. On the Continent the recruiting of more and more young girls eventually led to the exposure of the importation of girls from one country to another by unscrupulous officers employed under Regulation; while in England cruelties under the Acts were scandalous. The girls could be arrested and, under threat of forcible examination to prove or disprove virginity, were made to sign on as prostitutes.

Josephine made a list of accounts of innocent girls who had been forced into compulsory examination. Glen Petrie, in *A Singular Iniquity,* has alleged that some of these accounts were found to be false: 'Josephine, as so often happened, though she would never knowingly have countenanced dishonesty, was too impetuous, and too hard-worked, to verify every tale reported to her.' But he does go on to affirm that 'one, at least, was well authenticated: the case of Caroline Wyburgh, of Chatham', a case of which he gives a detailed account. It is of such a kind as to prove that there were very many others and that the girls would break down and give in rather than suffer more.

> 'Caroline was aged nineteen, lived in one room with her mother and kept them both by working at the most menial form of domestic service—scrubbing doorsteps and basement areas at a penny or two a time. She was generally held to be a good girl, sober, honest, industrious and never home late. She was also, and it was fatal, "walking out"

with a soldier. Late one night she was roused from her bed by an Inspector Wakeford of the Metropolitan Police (he was later to testify before the Royal Commission on the Contagious Diseases Acts saying, in answer to the question did he believe that a Common Prostitute was a woman who earned her livelihood by prostitution. "If you confine yourself to this definition your Acts will never succeed"). Inspector Wakeford insisted that she was a prostitute and that, despite the lateness of the hour, she should go up with him for examination. Caroline refused, saying "she was not one of that lot". Inspector Wakeford replied that if she persisted in her refusal he would make sure she spent three months at hard labour in Maidstone Gaol. At this, her mother, faced with the prospect of three months without Caroline's pitiful wage to support her, persuaded her to go. At the police station she was presented with a piece of paper and ordered, since she was illiterate, to make her mark. She did so, carefully stating at the same time that she "had always been a good girl". Since the paper was the form of "voluntary submission" her statement was ignored. She was then taken to the examination room. As soon as she saw the surgical couch with its tray of instruments, and the stock-like clamps which were used for bracing the legs of recalcitrant women, she refused absolutely to submit to examination. She was then dragged to one of the "Lock" wards, strapped into bed where she was kept for four days and subjected to a diet of black tea and dry bread. On the fifth day she agreed to be examined provided no instruments were used. As soon as she entered the surgery she was forced into a strait-jacket, thrust into the couch and her feet were clamped apart in the required position, while an assistant thrust his elbow on to her breasts to prevent her from struggling. Struggle she did, with the result that her body rolled out of the couch while her ankles remained secure in the stocks causing her serious injury. Meanwhile the blood which issued from between her legs told its own story. According to Caroline's mother, who was present at this edifying scene, the doctor laughed and said, "Well, now you can go home. You have been telling the truth. You are not a 'bad girl'." The matron of the "Lock" hospital took her to her office, gave her a hot dinner and presented her with five shillings after exacting from her a promise—which Caroline understandably decided not to keep—that she would never tell "any Lady or Gentleman" about what had occurred. It was such incidents as these which inspired W. T. Stead (Josephine's biographer and editor of the *Northern Echo* and later the *Pall Mall Gazette*) to describe compulsory surgical examination as "surgical rape".

'To this, Josephine added that she had seen hardened prostitutes having to be removed unconscious from the surgical couch after examination, while in one case she herself had witnessed, the patient, who was pregnant, had suffered a "flooding" of blood, and had lost her baby as a result.'

Glen Petrie, who in his book gives a sterling picture of social conditions at the time, finds Josephine 'impetuous' but not quite truthful in her disclosures. He excuses her for not being able to confirm all the stories told her. This attitude does not give the real picture. He makes a similar allegation in his account of Cowper-Temple asking Josephine if she had not been nervous at having to appear before the Royal Commission. Her reply, he tells us, was 'a trifle harsh and not entirely truthful'. That is his opinion but it could not be mine. If we go back to E. Moberly Bell's account of the incident which I have quoted in full on pages 31-34, the latter part of which Petrie omits, we shall see that far from being afraid of the members of the Commission, of whom Cowper-Temple was one, and who were for the most part hostile, she stood up to them bravely, and when Cowper-Temple sought to make a placatory remark, she gave him a straight answer and he acknowledged the truth of what she said. There is a great difference between being nervous and being indignant.

It might only be a hint, but there is, in what Petrie says, a suggestion of fear on Josephine's part. But she was not afraid —any more than St Paul was before Nero (the comparison is hers). She felt the clasp of a divine hand. Many of the members of the Commission would have hoped for fear; they received brave answers. For Josephine, the judgement of the Commission did not count; the demand for repeal would go on, and nothing less than repeal was acceptable to her.

If Josephine was not afraid, there were times when her friends were afraid for her and urged her away from impending actions and decisions. She would never allow herself to be swayed.

The greatest pressure was put upon her when she was threatened with legal action from Belgian officials at government level.

It had been discovered that English girls were being sold to brothels in Belgium and that Englishmen in high places were involved. Belgian law sanctioned prostitution, and brothels were recognised and taxed; but the law did forbid the admission of girls under the age of sixteen. The age of consent in England was still twelve. Josephine was told in Liège that 'waggon-loads of girls had been brought into Belgium'. The report haunted her and she was anxious to know the truth of it.

The Society of Friends asked two of its members, Alfred Dyer and George Gillett, to look into the matter. Early in 1880 they visited Brussels to investigate the cases of English girls, many of whom were minors, who were alleged to be detained in the licensed houses there against their will, and with the connivance of the police. A Belgian barrister was investigating on his own behalf the disappearance of an English girl, the sister of a friend of his. His search was unsuccessful, but in the course of it he had discovered much to horrify him. Josephine met these men in Brussels, in the company of one of her Belgian colleagues, Pastor Anet. They told her they had discovered that little girls of all nationalities between the ages of eleven and fifteen were enslaved there.

Some of these girls were rescued and brought to England where Josephine took them under her care. She wrote:

> 'Another of the poor refugees helped by Pastor Anet to escape from Brussels came to our house in Liverpool. She appeared to be in pain, and on being questioned she replied that she was suffering from unhealed stripes on her back and shoulders from the lash of this tyrant. I drew from her, when alone, the story of her martyrdom. The keeper of this house in Brussels, enraged with her because of her persistent refusal to participate in some exceptionally base proceedings among his clients, had her carried to an underground chamber, whence her cries could not be heard. She was here immured and starved, and several times scourged with a thong of leather. But she did not yield. This poor delicate girl had been neglected from childhood. She was a Catholic, but had had little or no religious teaching. She told me, with much simplicity, that in the midst of these tortures she was "all the time strengthened and comforted by the thought that Jesus had Himself been cruelly scourged, and that He could feel for her."'

Because it was illegal to have under-age girls in the brothels, the children were locked up and kept hidden, reserved for special clients. Brothel keepers and police frequently worked together.

Dyer and Gillett made a statement to the Procureur Général and also to the British authorities, with the result that the British were invited to send a delegation to see for themselves. The two Scotland Yard detectives who were sent were received with a great show of frankness by the Brussels police; they were taken to the brothels, from which the girls had already been secretly removed and, seeing no evidence of irregularity, returned satisfied that all was in order.

Colonel Vincent, Director of the Criminal Investigation Department, sent for Josephine and showed her the officers' reports. She was not convinced.

Later, in Paris where she was attending a meeting, she met a Belgian detective who was disgusted at what was going on in his country and was prepared to expose all he knew. He told her that Dyer and Gillett had left the Procureur du Roi very uneasy as a result of their allegations:

'He sent for Schraeder and asked "Is it true that you allow very young girls, and English &c. &c.?" Schraeder said "Oh, non, non, Monsieur." Then he rushed off to Lenaer's house (Lenaer is head of the whole police) and said "M. le Procureur asks *have we any minors?*" Lenaer turned livid and sank back in his armchair. After a bit he jumped up, and ordered two carriages. In ten minuets these carriages "brûlaient les rues de Bruxelles" flying along. They called at such and such infamous houses and carried off the minors who were there, and sent them with a detective *across the frontier*. Then the detective went back in a couple of hours to M. le Procureur du Roi and smilingly said "Perhaps M. le Procureur would come himself and walk through all the houses and see if there are any minors." '

M. le Procureur *did so*, and the next day, says Josephine, 'he wrote to our *Times* and *Standard* saying that our statements were entirely false'.

This gave Josephine all the evidence she needed and she obtained from the Belgian detective the names and addresses of all the people concerned.

The confidence with which she took up this defence of little girls who were bought for the use of evil men, and the determination of her attack on the highest authorities, show the extent of her trust in God and assurance of His power. She knew what was coming to her when in 1880 she published in *The Shield*, the Abolitionist newspaper, a plain statement that children as young as eleven were imprisoned in brothels in Brussels, where they were treated with great cruelty. The article was at once translated into French and published in the Belgian papers.

The fat was in the fire. Denials came from the Belgian police. English newspapers were deeply moved by Josephine's intemperate attack on a friendly neighbour. Pressure from Belgian authorities forced the hand of the Procureur Général who sent a formal demand to the Home Secretary in London, calling for a repeat statement under oath before a magistrate. There was the usual outburst from many of Josephine's friends who felt that this time she had gone too far, and appealed to her to withdraw. She was urged to 'do anything rather than open the Gates of Hell', which was seen as the inevitable result of her action. Benjamin Scott, Chamberlain of the City of London and long a supporter of the Repeal movement, sent a special messenger through the night to Liverpool. He arrived at 5 a.m. and knocked up the whole household. Josephine recorded:

'It was quite dark. I lighted my candle to see to read the letter, and Jane made a fire downstairs and prepared some tea etc. for the messenger who was shivering with cold. He was to return to London again by the first train. I felt a little confused in the cold dark morning, reading a mysterious letter from the Guildhall, which contained also a telegram in cypher from Brussels, warning me that there was some trap being laid for us, and probably some collusion between the police of London and that of Belgium.'

Josephine insisted on sticking by her accusations. She could not deny the truth: 'I am longing to make known in the most public way these terrible cases. We wish these iniquities to be known.' Accompanied by George, she went into Liverpool and made her deposition before the magistrate. It was sent to the Home Office and then to Belgium, and Josephine waited for Hell to break loose.

The sequel was that an Inquiry was ordered in Brussels. Belgian newspapers asked Josephine for a copy of the deposition and it was published in full. The result was great public indignation, and the dismissal of the chiefs of police. Yet

Josephine was to write twenty years later:

> 'The system of Government-patented regulated vice *continues to exist*, and the friends of Justice continue to work and wait.'

In London the result of the publicity was the formation by the City of London of an Association for the Suppression of the Traffic in Women and Girls, of which Benjamin Scott was the moving spirit. They agreed on a Public Inquiry which would force Parliament to take active steps to repress the trade. An approach was made to the Government in 1881. Josephine sent a letter to her husband to tell him of her part in the business: she had already written to Lord Granville, the Foreign Secretary, saying:

> 'I shall be in London for three days and will wait those three days *outside your door,* until Your Lordship chooses either to hear my petition, or to order my removal!' She told George: 'Lord Granville sent for me at once and said, "No need for your three days' siege—I have already given notice I shall move on May 30th for a Committee of the House of Lords".'

This was done, but the tone of the House of Commons was such that, although the Bill was passed through the Lords, it was shelved or talked out of the Commons.

Chapter 9

JOSEPHINE was equal to any attack on her own actions. But now people were getting at George and even suggesting that the College was running down. He was in fact overworking and under great pressure in the field of education. A rumour was started that he would be asked to resign. He badly needed a rest, and Josephine was deeply concerned about his health. Yet if he were to retire they would have been hard pressed to exist decently. Realising this, a group of friends led by Henry Wilson got up a subscription from well-wishers which when invested realised £200 a year.

The situation was saved when George was offered a Canonry at Winchester. Here he would be assured of rest and a secure income.

But for Josephine, her special work was always to be done, and Winchester being a military town, it was now very much on her doorstep. Before long she had set up a life-line for women and girls needing special care, in the form of a rest-house similar to one she had previously set up in Liverpool. Amélie Humbert, a woman after her own heart, came to help her in Winchester. Rebecca Jarrett, a former brothel keeper converted through the Salvation Army, was engaged to run the house. When she came to Josephine, she offered her entire savings, thirty sovereigns, to the work for Repeal. Wisely, Josephine suggested that she should use it to provide home comforts for the rest-house.

Rebecca was later to feature in the famous 'Maiden Tribute' case in which W. T. Stead set out to prove that children could be bought by men. She did her part well, but sadly became a scapegoat and suffered two years' imprisonment, to the great sorrow of Josephine and her friends. But she was a worthy Christian, and after doing her two years she served in the Salvation Army for the rest of her long life.

A change of Government brought new hope to the Abolitionists, but the Home Office, the India Office and the War Office were led by avowed Regulationists who adamantly opposed reform. Stansfeld was not given a seat in the Cabinet, and this left him free to take complete charge of the campaign for Abolition.

The new House reappointed the Select Committee and Josephine was called as a witness in May 1882. It was quite different from her experience before the Royal Commission ten years before. Though some still expressed shocked surprise that any 'woman who called herself a lady' could meddle with a subject so improper, most members now realised that Abolitionists were serious-minded people and must be heard. Six out of the fifteen members of the Committee were committed to Abolition. When Josephine's knowledge of certain areas she had not visited for some time was questioned, she replied with some reason that

> 'negro slavery was abolished in our British possessions by a body of persons in England who had never seen a negro slave. They took their stand upon the principle that slavery was wrong; we take our stand entirely and purely on the principle that the State must not regulate prostitution; and no results given to us from year to year, as they are, no reports of this present Committee will in any respect or in the smallest degree alter our position, because we take our stand upon principles which are eternal.'

Her dignity and obvious sincerity made, as always, a deep impression on her hearers. It was the power of the Spirit of God in her. She was never lost for the best and most penetrating words, and they flowed inspired.

The Committee consisted of nine Regulationists and six Abolitionists, and it voted accordingly. The majority report declared in favour of the Regulations, reaffirming their effectiveness in checking disease and the work of reclamation carried out by the agents. Strangely enough it reaffirmed the finding of the Commission in 1872 that the Special Police 'are not chargeable with any abuse of their authority, and have hitherto discharged a novel and difficult duty with moderation and caution'. Yet the Committee had before it the cases of Mrs Percy and Caroline Wyburgh and other examples of unanswerable abuse. In commending the Acts, the majority report expressed the opinion that it would be good to extend them throughout the country; but added that in view of the widespread feeling against them, it recommended that things should remain as they were. It was, however, upon the minority report that the House acted, but not yet.

Josephine continued to canvass influential opinion. She paid a visit to Oxford where she looked up some old friends. The warden of Keble, Dr Talbot, was puzzled that she should want to discuss this particular subject. But she told him:

'It is fully time, I think, to come to Oxford and to Keble College when I get letters frequently from men dated "Keble College Oxford" beseeching me to give them instruction and to guide their bewildered minds to a little light on this great social problem.' She recorded: 'He started as if he was shot, and said, "What! Do my boys write to you?" "Yes", I said, "they do, and many other *boys* as well. They want some thoroughly truthful and manly instruction on this question, and they claim that they can best get it by writing to a woman." ' Poor Talbot!

She then went to see Scott Holland,

'a saint . . . learned and eloquent and rather subtle. I am not sure about him, though he eagerly listened. He looked as if a message from Heaven had been thundered at him and said "What shall we do?" '

Josephine did not enjoy her visit to Oxford. The older men had not changed their attitudes since her day. She reflected:

'How far back some men are. Fancy Talbot saying to me, "but do you really think that the sin is equal in men and women?" and some Archdeacon said to Rawlinson, "But you know it is absurd to suppose that the Seventh Commandment is binding on men as it is on women." I felt plainly the first few minutes with many of these men that they thought of me like Canon Liddon as "that dreadful woman Mrs Butler". This feeling adds to the pain and difficulty of such interviews.'

The only comfort she felt in Oxford was from 'those two good women Mrs Rolleston and Mrs Rawlinson who will pray and carry on the little bits I began'. But she had done more. She had made a change in Talbot's outlook; when Ellice Hopkiss was founding the White Cross League, Talbot invited her to address a meeting in Oxford and he took the chair.

It was Josephine's prayer life that gave her so much strength and surety of direction. In this she found the Society of Friends a tremendous help. For her their gentle faith and long sessions of silent prayer held the secret of spiritual power. In 1883 the Friends invited Christians of all denominations to a two-day Prayer Convention at their headquarters at Bishopsgate, when corporate prayer was to be offered for the success of the campaign for Abolition. There were more meetings for men and women in East London and finally there was a great meeting at Exeter Hall presided over by Benjamin Scott. Those who attended from the provinces went back to organise prayer meetings at home. The whole country was at prayer.

In Parliament, Hopwood had put down a motion condemning the compulsory examination of women, which was to follow the Debate on the Address. Josephine took a room at the Westminster Palace Hotel where she arranged for continuous prayer to be offered throughout the day and as far into the night as the House might sit. Clergy of various denominations came in turn to conduct services of intercession and between these were periods of silent prayer. The room was crowded. Some men were present, but most were women, women of all sorts,

> 'well dressed ladies, some even of high rank, kneeling together (almost side by side) with the poorest, and some of the outcast women of the purlieus of Westminster'.

While the prayer continued, Josephine went backwards and forwards between the hotel and the lobby of the House, where younger members expressed embarrassment at the thought of 'all those women praying for them'.

Hopwood was unable to introduce his motion. But on April 20th, Stansfeld was more fortunate. He proposed 'that this House disapproves the compulsory examination of women under the Contagious Diseases Acts'. Josephine tells us what happened:

> 'All day long groups had met for prayer—some in the houses of MPs, some in churches, some in halls, where the poorest people come. Meetings were being held all over the kingdom, and telegraphic messages of sympathy came to us continually from Scotland and Ireland, France, Switzerland and Italy. There was something in the air like the approach of victory. As men and women prayed, they suddenly burst forth into praise, thanking God for the answer, as if it had already been granted. It was a long debate. The tone of the speeches, both for and against, was remarkably purified and, with one exception, they were altogether on a higher plane than in former debates. Many of us ladies sat through the whole evening till after midnight; then came the division. A few minutes previously Mr Gerard, the steward of the Ladies Gallery, crept quietly in and whispered to me: "I think you are going to win."

That reserved official, of course, never betrays sympathy with any party; nevertheless I could see the irrepressible pleasure in his face when he said this.

'Never can I forget the expression on the faces of our MPs in the House when they all streamed back from the Division lobby. The interval during their absence had seemed very long and we could hear each other breathing so deep was the silence. We did not require to wait to hear the announcement of the division by the tellers; the faces of our friends told the tale. Slowly and steadily they pressed in headed by Mr Stansfeld and Mr Hopwood, the tellers on our side. Mr Fowler's face was beaming with joy and a kind of humble triumph. I thought of the words "Say unto Jerusalem her warfare is accomplished". It was a victory of righteousness over gross selfishness, injustice and deceit and for the moment we were all elevated by it. When the figures were given out a long-continued cheer arose, which sounded like a Psalm of praise. Then we ran quickly down from the gallery and met a number of our friends coming out from Westminster Hall.

'It was half-past one in the morning and the stars were shining in the clear sky. I felt at that silent hour in the morning the spirit of the Psalmist who said: "When the Lord turned again the captivity of Zion, we were like unto them that dream", it almost seemed like a dream.'

The voting for the Repeal was 182 to 110 and the Government suspended the Acts in the following month.

Chapter 10

IT is easier to give a straightforward account of Josephine Butler's life work than to enter with appreciation and understanding into the depth of her prayer life. Yet to do so would be to ignore the true source of her strength. A depth of prayer such as hers is all too rare in the world, particularly in the spiritually impoverished Britain of today.

She read widely about prayer, and her reading crossed all denominational divisions. She was moved to compare Bernard of Clairvaux with the young, hard-working ministers and other Christian workers of her day:

'Bernard of Clairvaux, when engaged in a correspondence with persons and orders throughout the whole of Europe, battling single-handed with an amount of work which might overwhelm any modern Secretary of State, found that on the days when he spent the most time in prayer, and in listening to the voice of God and the teachings of the Spirit, his letters were the most rapidly written and persuasive, and his active work the most promptly and successively accomplished. His many schemes, evolved from his own ingenious brain, widened into or were lost in the far greater plan and purpose of God; anxiety was allayed; power—the power of the Holy Spirit, to which he had opened his heart—flowed forth, and was felt in every word he wrote or spoke, and in his very presence and looks.'

Of Oberlin, she wrote that he

'reserved stated hours for private prayer during the day, at which times none, as a rule, were permitted to interrupt him. These hours came to be known to all his parishioners, and it was usual for carters or labourers, returning from the fields with talk and laughter, to uncover their heads as they passed beneath the walls of his house. If the children ran by too noisily these working people would check them with uplifted finger, and say, "Hush! He is praying for us." At times his soul was moved to an agony of intercession for his people; he travailed in birth for them. Sometimes he was in darkness on their account. His natural kindness to all becoming, under the influence of the Holy Spirit, a constant yearning and desire for their salvation, he would spend hours on his knees pouring out his soul in prayer for them with "strong crying and tears". He felt the awful nature of the responsibility of one who is called to be an overseer of the flock of God, and who must give an account of the souls committed to him. "Oh, my people, my children, my friends! " he would cry in his prayers—apostrophising them, and pleading *with* them as well as for them, though he was alone with God.'

Josephine was drawn to Catherine of Siena because of Catherine's depth and simplicity in prayer. She quotes from the *Dialogue of Catherine*:

'Perfect prayer, then consists not in the multitude of words, but in the strength of the desire which raises the soul towards God . . . Every Christian ought to contribute towards the salvation of souls, according as he is inspired by a holy desire. Everything which is said and done for the salvation of men is a continual prayer, but a prayer which does not exempt us from the use of mental and vocal prayer at certain times. All that is done for the love of God and of our neighbour, all, it may be added, which is done for ourselves also, with a just and a right aim, may be called prayer, for those never cease to pray who never cease to do good. Love for our fellow-creatures is a constant prayer;

but this very love will always invite us to actual prayer at stated seasons, and for prescribed times and even far beyond those prescribed times, if the salvation of a soul, or any emergency in which we find ourselves demands it.'

The more she studied Catherine, the more Josephine felt a kinship with her. She wrote:

'Those who have any experience of real prayer know full well that in the pause of the soul before God, after it has uttered its complaint, made known its desires, or sought guidance in perplexity, there comes the clearer vision of duty, and the still small voice of guidance is heard, rectifying the judgement, strengthening the resolve, and consoling the spirit; they know that influence external to us yet within us, deals with us, speaks with us, in fire. Prayer cannot be truly called commission, if the only voice heard be the voice of the pleader.'

She said further of Catherine:

'She shrank from no toil nor pains nor sacrifice in order that she might find and win Christ, and be found in Him; and thus she might bring blessing to man. Her philosophy was based on a deep humility, and a conviction of the weakness and sinfulness of man. Yet she perceived and realised withal—that which many who talk loudly of progress and the perfectibility of the human race do not see—*the beauty and worth of every human soul, even in the midst of its utmost ignorance and bondage to sin.* She loved, she prayed, she endured. She fought a good fight, and she fell in the heat of the battle, vanquished, and yet a conqueror. When Urban angrily reproached them [the cardinals] with their profligacy and with the misery they caused to the poor (for he appears to have had a real sympathy with the humble classes of people) they replied with the usual hypocritical cant, that "vices of the kind alluded to with such painful and unseemly plainness of speech by the Pontiff had existed from the beginning of the world, and must always exist; that Moses, the great lawgiver had wisely provided for and legislated for these evils, thus recognising them as a perpetual necessity of human society, that all men and still more all women were frail; that it was utopian to pretend that immorality could be rooted out; that Christianity itself had never done anything towards purifying society of the evil indicated by the Pontiff and that those men and women who were generally considered to be saints would be seen to be, in fact, no better than others, could the secrets of their lives be known." '

The final bitter comment of the cardinals was, of course, directed at Catherine at whose instigation Urban was attacking the corruption of the cardinals and the Church. As Josephine wrote this of Catherine and her times, she must have had her own opponents in mind. She goes on:

'No amount of wickedness appalled her [Catherine] into the belief that any sinners must be left to perish as outcasts of God and hope. In her last exhortations to her friends she bade them hope for all "for there is no man on earth," she said, "however wicked, who may not repent and live." '

Josephine herself had no doubt that the reforms for which she fought for so long were brought about by the power of prayer. Speaking of the changed atmosphere in the House of Commons at the Repeal debate and motion, she observed:

'There is a distinct change of tone in the House and we believe it dates from the time we came forward to claim God as our Leader. Our cause was openly baptised, so to speak, in the name of Christ and our advance has been steady ever since. Also I thought I saw what I had never observed before in the sceptical and worldly atmosphere of

Parliament, i.e. signs of a consciousness of a spiritual strife going on. Some Members spoke to us of a spiritual power in our movement, while on the other hand there is a seething and boiling of unworthy passions such as would appal one if one did not remember that it was when the great Incarnation of purity drew near the possessed man of old that the unclean spirits cried out . . . We have arranged for a great meeting of prayer, we shall hold it close to the House of Commons . . .'

Millicent Fawcett and E. M. Turner record in their commemorative *Life and Work of Josephine Butler:*

'No one but the possessor of extraordinary spiritual power could have won such a victory. Such power was in the most eminent degree Mrs Butler's. Hardly anyone could come in contact with her without feeling it; and I hope I am not presumptuous when in my own mind, I apply to her, words that were spoken by and of Another: "This sort goeth not forth but by prayer and fasting." '

All her life, Josephine showed a natural, unassuming sanctity. At the early age of seventeen she was moved by prayer to plead with God, question God, on behalf of mankind. Carrying 'the call', she found her way, under God, through hazards and horrors of the basest kind, to champion and rescue women and children. Confronting the power of a strong and prejudiced government she gathered support and fought for many years to break down the strongly-held attitudes which resulted in heedless cruelty to poor ignorant women and girls. Of the government itself she never ceased to demand the repeal and undoing of unjust laws.

The word compassion is a big and beautiful one. It involves more than pity, more than feeling the sorrows of others. It involves experiencing the pain of their sorrow and suffering as if it were one's own. Josephine once spoke of feeling 'fierce', and it was the personal violation she suffered; she felt it as if it were done to her. She suffered the terrors of helpless women wrongfully arrested and accused. She was shut up in a room like the innocent mites waiting to be ravished by evil men. With that compassion she said some beautiful things:

'The Human Society towards which it is our duty to strive, will have within it no human dregs. The Law which it will obey will be, in deed and truth, Common Law embracing within its retaining, guiding arms, every man and every woman, and will be administered with justice to all, but with special forbearance and tenderness to the poor, the weak and friendless.

'I believe that a time is coming when it will be apparent that the principle for which we are contending—the unity of the moral law, and the equality of all human souls before God—is the most fruitful and powerful revolutionising principle which the world has ever known, and that we shall achieve a victory in the course of years, and through much tribulation, which will make our present efforts seem trivial for the attainment of so great an end.'

Some of the sayings of Josephine are outstanding for all time and deeply moving, poetic and profound, though simple. This one is pure music:

'I feel called upon to press upon your hearts,
 Love to the fallen, the outcasts,
 Even the madly sinful,
 Love to every human being however degraded
 Who bears the impress of the Divine image.'

By her own example it is seen that she lived that kind of life and loved in that sort of way. Read again:

'There is no evil in the world so great that God cannot raise up to meet it a corresponding beauty and glory that will blaze it out of countenance.'

Again:

'The awful abundance of compassion that makes me fierce.'

In Josephine's numerous speeches and writings no words are wasted and she gave to each its full weight and meaning. She was wonderfully gifted. It is refreshing to feel her steady assurance of God in every letter she wrote and in every speech she made, especially when these are placed alongside the self assurance of today's humanists, many of whom are good people, but they work from a limited base. One of our leading Christians today, Bishop Trevor Huddleston, has described himself as 'a Christian Humanist'. So it was with Josephine. It was God in her who wrote and spoke.

In the same year after the Repeal, she gave a talk in Birmingham entitled 'The Bright Side of the Question'. Here are two paragraphs which show how close her mind was to God and prayer:

'I will say then to the women here one word. Dear women, I recall a scene; you will understand me. The night of the memorable debate in April, lasting many hours, there were meetings of women not far from the House of Commons, where I was in the Ladies' Gallery, and joined those meetings for a few minutes. It was a sight I shall never forget. At one meeting there were the poorest, most ragged and miserable women from the slums of Westminster on their knees before the God of Hosts with tears and groans pouring out the burden of their sad hearts. He alone knew what that burden was. There were mothers who had lost daughters; there were sad-hearted women; and side by side with these poor souls, dear to God as we are, there were ladies of high rank, in their splendid dresses—Christian ladies of the upper classes kneeling and also weeping. I thank God for this wonderful solidarity of the women of the world before God. Women are called to be a great power in the future, and by this terrible blow which fell upon us forcing us to leave our privacy and bind ourselves together for our less fortunate sisters, we have passed through an education—a noble education. God has prepared in us, in the women of the world, a force for all future causes which are great and just.

'We shall not stop, our efforts will not cease when this particular struggle is at an end. God has called us out, and we must not go back from any warfare to which He will now call us in the future. We praise, we thank Him for what He has done already for us, and for what He is going to do, for we shall one day have a complete victory. We can echo the words of that which is written: "My soul doth magnify the Lord, and my spirit hath rejoiced in God my Saviour, for He hath regarded the low estate of His handmaidens." And, remember, women, if we are faithful unto death, from henceforth all men shall call us blessed. Yes, generations to come, your children and your children's children will call you blessed, because you have laboured for purer morals and for juster laws.'

Josephine's fight on behalf of her fellow women did not end with the Repeal. A short speech at the City Temple on July 20th, 1891 shows her pressing the importance of Women's Suffrage; but her stance is a godly one.

'I am sorry that fear and timidity are growing up again and that a fresh conspiracy of silence threatens us. God gives us phraseology, a pure and chaste and holy indignation, which makes it possible for us to go to the bottom of these things without offending the chastest ear. For twenty-one years I have worked with my dear fellow-workers in a public manner against these hateful laws, which one of the resolutions pronounced and which I pronounce accursed. During these twenty-one years there was one thing which made our battle harder than it would have been. We have had to fight outside the Constitution. We have been knocking at the door of the Constitution all these years, and there are men who even now tell me that they would give us anything in the way of justice except the Parliamentary vote. We have been talking about certain Members of Parliament who are not fit to occupy that position. Give the women a vote and see what will be the result. In all my work my one strength has been the strength of the Almighty, sought and won by constant prayer; and the prayer which I now offer in my secret chamber is that the veil may be taken away and the selfishness—the perhaps unconscious selfishness—may be removed from the hearts of men who deny women equality, and keep them outside the Constitution. Think what we could do in the cause of morality, think of the pain and trouble and martyrdom that we might be saved in the future, if we had that little piece of justice.'

Josephine's voice must have been one of the first to call for the vote for women. In 1892 she wrote:

'We may pray and we may preach about these things, and we may raise our voices to some little extent during the excitement of a contested election; but that is not enough. My friends we must have the suffrage. It is our right and it is cruel, and continued injustice to withhold it from us. It has lately been said that the women generally of the country have not shown any desire for the suffrage. Some years ago I can assert that the women of the country showed a very great desire for it. Men do not know that at the bottom of that desire underneath many other good motives, there lies a bitterness of woe which is the most powerful stimulus towards the desire for representation in the Legislature. I am sometimes afraid that one of these days some other terrible injustice may be enacted in Parliament through which women will suffer as they did under those laws I have alluded to. Perhaps it might not be an altogether bad thing, if it caused women to utter once more the bitter cry to which none of the legislators could pretend to be deaf. But have we not, as it is, sufficient trouble, and misery, and degradation among our own sex to make us utter even now the bitter cry—a cry however at the same time of hope, courage and confidence.'

One of her greatest concerns was to encourage more women workers, where too few found it easy to say, 'Here am I, send me.' It is good to read of how the American Dr Kate Bushnell was guided to join the battle against Regulation. She was turning over the leaves of her Bible and turned to Joseph's dream. From that she found herself reading of Belshazzar's dream and Daniel's interpretation. Again she turned to St Matthew's Gospel. There she read how after Herod's death the Lord appeared in a dream to Joseph in Egypt. Baffled and weary, she said to the Lord, 'I am so stupid in understanding His guidance.' Then she fell asleep and almost instantly was herself dreaming: 'I felt myself tossed on the billows of the Atlantic on my way to England to see Josephine Butler.' Josephine recalls that 'at this time we had never met nor corresponded'. Dr Bushnell wrote to Josephine, who replied that she and her friends had been praying that God would raise up an English-speaking woman to go to India to enquire into conditions regarding the abolition of Regulation there. So the first step was taken which led to the eventual passing in 1895 of an act which prohibited all examination or registration of women in the Indian cantonments.

Josephine never tired of meditating on the Scriptures. She was gripped by the drama of Hagar and Sarah and in 1894 she published *The Lady of Shunam*. With her mind as always on the lowly and the unwanted, she wrote:

'Is it not though, a fact which should wake up the whole Christian world to a truer and clearer view of life as it is around us, that the first record of a direct communication from Jehovah to a woman is this of His meeting with the rejected Hagar, alone in the wilderness? It is not with Sarah the princess, or any other woman, but with Hagar, the ill-used slave, that the God of Heaven stooped to converse, and to whom He brought His supreme comfort and guidance. This fact has been to me a strength and consolation in confronting the most awful problem on earth i.e. the setting apart for destruction, age after age, of a vast multitude of women—of those whom we dare call lost—beyond all others lost—hopelessly lost. We ourselves by our utmost efforts, have only so far been able to save a few, a mere handful among the multitude; and of the others, unreached by any divinely-inspired *human* help, we are apt to think with dark and dismal foreboding. We forget that though they might be quite beyond the reach of our helping hands, they are never beyond the reach of His hand—His, who "being put to death in the flesh" was "quickened by the Spirit, by which also He went and preached to the spirits in prison".

'Into the vilest prison-houses on earth (I believe) He descends *alone* many a time, to save those souls buried out of the sight and ken of His servants and ministers, even as He—He alone, unaccompanied by any chosen ministers—descended into Hades and "preached the Gospel also to those that are dead" that they who have been "judged according to men in the flesh" may "live according to God in the Spirit".'

I cannot end this expression of my devotion to Josephine Butler without quoting her own words in which she looks at herself, and her husband George, after his death. I pray that my readers may feel the beauty of her thoughts and words. For me they are both deep and simple.

'To speak of clouded moments of one's own life involves no small effort. But in justice both to my husband and to the movement I have tried to serve I am impelled to do so. There are some people who, if they remember at all that moral uprising against national unrighteousness in which we took part, still regard it as an illusion, and its advocacy as a "fad", or even as a blot on an otherwise inoffensive career—something which must always require explanation or apology. But there are others who understood from the first its true meaning and far-reaching issues, and who have perhaps imagined that an unbroken consistency of action, based on an immovable strength of conviction, must at all times have characterised any man or woman destined to take a representative part in it. A sense of justice forces me to confess that the fact (in regard to myself) was not always as they imagined; for there was a time when I resembled the faint-hearted though loyal disciple who, when venturing to walk on the waters, in an evil moment looked away from Christ and around upon the weltering, unstable floor on which he stood, and immediately began to sink. When moreover the sense of justice of which I speak regards one who was and is dear to me as my own soul, then I am doubly forced to speak, and to give "honour to whom honour is due" by telling of the wisdom which God gave him in encouraging and supporting through a few troubled years the tried and wavering advocate of a cause in which both faith and courage were put to a severe test.

'A deeply-rooted faith—a personal, and not merely a traditional faith—in the central truths of Christ, and moral strength, the fruit of that faith, were in him united with other qualities which were needful for the task he so well fulfilled. Others whom I have known—teachers and fathers in God—have had this moral and spiritual faith in a high degree, together with an eloquence and power in argument to which he had no pretension. But few—it seemed to me at least—possessed such patience as he had, such long-suffering, such a power of silent waiting, such a dignified reserve, and such a strong respect for individuality as to forbid all probing of inner wounds, or questioning of motive or action, even in the case of one so near to him as myself. He had great delicacy and refinement in dealing with the bitterness or petulance of a soul in trouble. He had great faith in his fellow-creatures. And these, together with his unfailing love, like the sun in the heavens surmounting the hours of cold and darkness, gradually overcame the mists which had wrapped themselves round the heart and obscured the spiritual vision of her for whom he never ceased to pray.

'At this time his voice, when simply reading the words of Christ at family prayers, used to sound in my ears with a strange and wonderful pathos, which pierced the depths of rebellious or despairing thought. At times his attitude—probably unconsciously to himself—assumed in my eyes an unaccustomed and almost awful sternness. Sometimes my unrest of mind found vent in words of bitterness (which however only skimmed the surface of the inward trouble), and I waited for him to speak. Then he seemed to rise before me to a stature far above my level, above that of other men, and even above his own at other times, while he gently led me back to the great first principles and to the Source of all Truth, presenting to me, in a way which I could sometimes hardly bear the perfection and severity of the law of God, and our own duty in patient obedience and perseverance, even when the ascent is steepest, and the road darkest and longest. He very seldom gave me direct personal advice or warning. He simply stood there before me in the light of God, truthful, upright, single-minded; and all that had been distorted or wrong in me was rebuked by that attitude alone; and a kind of peace, rather than actual peace, entered my soul, and my heart replied, "Where you stand now, beloved, I shall also stand again one day, perhaps soon, on firm ground, and in the light of God." And my soul bowed in reverence before him, although never could he bear any outward expression of that reverence. It seemed to hurt him. He would gently turn away from it. He spoke firmly when he differed from any doubtful sentiment expressed or argument used. His simple "no", or "I think you are wrong," were at times more powerful to me, than the most awful pulpit denunciation or argumentative demonstration of my error could have been; and then, even if he condemned, his love and reverence never failed.

'He knew the psalms almost by heart, and the inspired words which he always had so ready were more potent for me, when spoken by him, than any other thing. His religion, and his method of consoling, were not of a subtle or philosophical kind, and he was all the better of a comforter to me because he did not—perhaps could not—easily enter into and follow all the windings of my confused thinkings and doubtings and revolted feelings. Strong swimmer as he was, I felt in my half-drowned state his firm grasp, and his powerful stroke upon the waters as we neared the land; and when by his aid my feet stood once more upon the solid rock, I understood the full force of the grateful acknowledgement of the Psalmist, "Thou hast kept my feet from falling, and mine eyes from tears." . . .

'I have not up till now dwelt upon the wrongs and sorrows which we were forced deliberately to look upon and measure, nor shall I do so. Could I do so, my readers would not wonder at any suffering or distress of brain caused by such a subject of contemplation. Dante tells us that when, in his dream, he entered the Inferno and met its sights and sounds, he fell prone "as one dead". I once replied to a friend, who complained of my using strong expressions and asked the meaning of them, as follows: "Hell hath opened her mouth. I stand in the near presence of the powers of evil. What I see and hear are the smoke of the pit, the violence of the torture inflicted by man on his fellows, the cries of lost spirits, the wail of the murdered innocents, and the laughter of demons." But these, it will be said, are mere figures of speech. So they are, used purposely to cover—for no words can adequately express—the reality which they symbolise. But the reality is there, not in any dream or poetic vision of woe, but present on this earth; hidden away, for the most part, from the virtuous and the happy, but not from the eyes of God. Turning from the contemplation of such unspeakable woes and depths of moral turpitude, it was a strength and comfort beyond description, through the years of strife, to look upon the calm face of my best earthly friend. It was a peace-imparting influence. And now that I walk alone and look only at his portrait, even that seems to take me into the presence of God, where he now dwells among the "spirits of just men made perfect", and to whisper hope of the approaching solution of the great mystery of sin and pain.

'I often recall an incident, which occurred at Winchester in the cathedral, a trifle in itself, but which dwells in my memory as an illustration of the help he gave me spiritually in time of need. It was during the service on Sunday. I suddenly felt faint, the effect of a week of unusual effort and hard work. Wishing not to disturb anyone or make a scene, I took the opportunity, when all heads were bowed in prayer, to creep down from the stalls as silently as possible, past the tomb of William Rufus, and down the choir, holding on when possible by the carved woodwork of the seats. A moment more, and I should have dropped. I could scarcely steady my steps, and my sight failed, when suddenly there passed a flash of light, as it seemed, before my eyes, something as white as snow and as soft as an angel's wing; it enveloped me, and I felt myself held up by a strong, loving arm, and supported through the nave to the west door, where the cool summer breeze restored me. It was my husband. He was in his own seat near the entrance to the nave, and his quick ear had caught the sound of my footstep. Quite noiselessly he left his seat and took me in his arms, unobserved by anyone. The flash of light (the angel's wing) was the quick movement of the wide sleeve of his fine linen surplice, upon which the sun shone as he drew me towards him.'

George was Josephine's confidant and confessor. She was ever conscious of his delicacy of approach, his patient, long-suffering, silent waiting, and his strong respect for her individuality which forbade any probing—'even in the case of one so near to him as myself'. I believe that George knew full well he was trying to guide a saint. For the most part he remained silent when she was torn and tried, content to be her sounding board against which she answered her own questions. She spoke to him as she spoke to God, and it was not for him to reply; God had to give her the answers, and it was clear that He did.

Nearing seventy, she wrote:

'I thank God that I long ago got far beyond being taunted with youth, and suspected of an enthusiasm which is a mere ardour of the blood, untried by experience of life. The sweet visions of my early youth, when I used to sit under the shade of the trees in my father's home and read of the holy martyrs and dream of a golden age, are nothing compared with the hope and enthusiasm which God gives me now, and which He has continued to give me while health failed, and some present hopes were blighted, and my way began to be strewn with the graves of those I loved, and I trod the lonely path of widowhood, and the world's worst evils continued to glare in my eyes. I have had sharp, deep wounds and long conflict of soul; but *now* ought not I, if anyone ought, to tell out the hopes which God gives me, and to speak of the ever-widening horizon which I see illumined by His redeeming love?

"Return unto thy rest, O my soul;
For the Lord hath dealt bountifully with thee." '

Looking back, as an old woman, she could say:

'I have often had occasion, in the course of many years of arduous work, again and again to meet groups of my fellow workers, especially on the Continent, who have confessed themselves subjected to periods of deep depression and disappointment. Having gone through the same experience myself and having been driven back upon God again and again, when everything seemed dark and hopeless, He has taught me some precious lessons which I have been called to impart sometimes to others. The central truth to which I have learned to hold fast is this truth—that death must precede resurrection; and that in every cause which is truly God's cause failures and disappointments are not only familiar things but even necessary for final success of the cause. *It is the lesson of the Cross.* The spirit of the poor disciples walking on the road to Emmaus who said "We trusted that it had been He who should have redeemed Israel" is a true picture of the experience of every true reformer. But when God has Himself led us into some of His secrets, and the inner meaning of His providential guidings, we no longer despond; for we come to know that it is a law in the Kingdom of Grace that death must precede resurrection. "Except a corn of wheat fall into the ground and die, it abideth alone; but if it die, it bringeth forth much fruit." For many years past therefore, I have been able, by God's grace, not only to acquiesce in apparent failure time after time, but even in a measure to rejoice, knowing that the way is thus being prepared, both in our own hearts and in the outward circumstances, for a more complete victory in the end.'

Towards the end of their centenary book on Josephine's *Work and Principles,* Millicent G. Fawcett and E. M. Turner tell us that:

'Josephine Butler's last public act was the writing of letters either of greeting or farewell to many of those who had been her collaborators in the great work of her life. In her own words she says she did not wish to belong to "a clique of pious people with no width of view"; "I have seen," she wrote, "many just men who gave life-long labour to casting out the evil spirits of tyranny, oppression and injustice: and of these, whatever their formula of belief may have been, the judge of all the world will say 'Well done.' " '

After recording her peaceful end in her sleep and the place of her burial at Kirknewton, they add these words as an epilogue:

'The seed which she has sown can never die.'

Chapter 11

IT is with reluctance that I turn from the words and work of Josephine Butler to the situation as it is today, with our economic and social conditions seemingly so much better. We ought to have learned so much more from the past. Yet we seem to have made retrograde use of our material gains and ease from poverty.

I would like to try to measure the conditions under which Josephine Butler fought, against our progress in a hundred years. Our 'progress' would seem to be towards profligacy, and little detail is needed to prove it. There is a call for more sexual freedom and fewer legal restrictions for the young. It is suggested that it should no longer be a criminal offence for a man to live on the immoral earnings of a woman. There are many who would like to put the clock back. We read in our papers of towns like Southampton, Birmingham and Leicester wanting special brothel areas; and like many of the bishops and clergy of a hundred years ago, some present day clergy support this idea. They think, no doubt, that the police, perhaps special police, would see to it that prostitutes were kept in the brothels and prevented from violating the better areas of the town. Today there is much that women will not tolerate, but one thing a brothel area would enforce is restriction, which would mean virtual imprisonment, with freedom of movement limited to within the area of the brothels.

We have learned from the horrors which Josephine Butler fought against, as we can learn from our newspapers today, what sort of people brothel keepers are—both men and women —and their hangers-on. They are loathsome. I emphasise this because the Christian people who think special brothel areas would be a good way of keeping their own areas clean, will be disappointed.

Men and women who live off prostitutes and prostitution are always on the look out for new recruits. The White Slave traffic is not dead, and all the old tricks are still used to entice young girls into prostitution. An attractive girl is worth procuring, shutting up, being forced to obey; and when used professionally, she will be shadowed round the clock, so that she can never escape. The slavery is still very real, as is the punishment and the torture should she try to get away.

Personal experience must carry weight in argument; it was so with Josephine Butler and it is so with me. I have often said that when I was spat at full in the face by a man and was able to take it without resentment, I felt closer to Christ than ever before. Yet perhaps I have felt even closer to Him when I have been in the company of my prostitute friends.

As I read the Bible story, I see in my imagination the Magdalene trying to attract Jesus; and His kindness in showing her what purity was—sending her to sell up her bits and pieces, her pictures and her tapestries, all that meant anything to her; so that her friends thought she had gone mad, and her customers pleaded with her in vain. Then with the money she got from the sale of her things, going to the best and most expensive shop she knew for the best bottle of balm —the best, the best, the best. Surely she must have been stopped by Simon's servants if she was a cheap tart? Yet she walked in on the men's meal. They would be sitting with their feet tucked behind them. Mary walked round to the Master's feet and wept as she silently knelt, broke open the bottle and gave every penny she had possessed—and from then on possessed more than she could ever calculate.

Cable Street in Stepney could tell its stories of those whom society commonly considers the lowest. A call from a café: 'Have a cup of tea with me, Father,' cried a girl who had nothing to pay for it with. It was my company, my kindness, my understanding, my charity—in short, Christ in me—that she needed and she knew she would get it. Or again, a wailing cry: 'Don't pass me by, Father,' from a young, unstable prostitute whom I might have avoided. She needed help and she needed a sympathetic, honest listener. Or again, the young woman dying of tuberculosis in a hospital ward, her way of life known well enough by the other patients for her to be shunned and condemned by them. A simple, friendly approach brought tears of gratitude to her eyes.

While there can be no measure of sin, so that no one can be justified in throwing stones at all, pride and prudery can be a particularly unrealised sickness. As a priest, going round my parish in my cassock, I knew and was befriended by prostitutes. I was always at home with them, and in a most gracious way I was humbly respected. I saw their tears and heard about their troubles and their hopes. I cursed their lives as they cursed them themselves. I have felt in my own body the kicks and punches they received from the men who lived on their earnings. I have suffered with them.

Whereas, in the last century, the privileged women and girls were protected while the men of their class used twelve-year-old girls and kept the brothels going, nowadays all men are equal and, we might say, there are more men to indulge and therefore more women and girls are at risk.

A recent case involving well-known personalities showed us how young girls could be trapped, used and enslaved by a vicious and clever woman prostitute. But even she could not outdo the men who trade and live on the immoral earnings of girls. A young girl brave enough to run away from such a man against the threat of having her parents' home burned down, told the judge how she was forced under water in a bath until she submitted to the man's wishes. But, for one brave girl, there are hundreds who are beaten into servitude. We are thinking in present day terms, when the age of consent is sixteen; but in April 1976 a judge heard the case of a man of thirty-seven who had been living on the immoral earnings of a girl of fifteen. He described the girl as 'a slave to the accused, who beat her savagely if she disobeyed him'.

Not only were the girl's prostitution and circumstances known, but the offences were committed under the eyes of social service officials while she was in the care of a council home, and this was admitted in court. The judge criticised the social services for not stopping the affair. Further, the girl was found to be four months pregnant.

Our social services are supposed to do better than the amateur Christian rescue work of old; they are trained to do the job. When social work was elevated to the level of a science, I stated publicly the shortcomings as I saw them in Stepney. The outstanding weakness was in the limited hours of work—only in the daylight hours—and the shut down over the weekends when help was needed most. I urged that shift work was needed, right round the clock. Without wishing to be offensive in any way, I wonder if the right kind of care can ever be given as it should be without the full Christian motivation—thinking and putting ourselves in the place of others. Josephine Butler said much the same thing a hundred years ago in her speech to the Royal Commission, and admitted, as I do today, the great difficulty of obtaining a sufficient supply of willing and dedicated workers.

Trained or untrained, paid or unpaid, to be any good we must be where people are. Only to prove and explain what I mean, I quote a letter, of which I feel unworthy, which I recently received from a woman who has been through most of the horrors of prostitution, and overcome them. She now lives a simple, hard life.

'My Dear, Dear Father Joe

How are you keeping? I am always thinking about you. I have written to you but have not heard from you for months and months. I hope all is going well for you, may the good Lord bless and care for you. I am struggling along —still doing a few hours at Art College—and most important of all keeping on the right side of God. I would love to come for a day and see you once again, but the rail fares are so high. You were so good to me in the past—both you and your dear wife. I was so lucky in my good friends. All I can say is, bless, bless and bless you—never stop praying for me dear Father Joe and always think well of me as I do you.

Regards and love, love and love . . .'

My friend will forgive me for quoting her; it is a joy to be so involved with people, and so close, and to be subject to such thoughts. It is most important to keep contact, and so a letter of that kind must be dealt with carefully and soon, as in this case, with the promise of a meeting which must be kept. The kind of care to be given is family care, belonging.

Like Josephine Butler, my concern has been for the prostitutes who are used and abused by evil men. There was another matter about which she felt deeply, and which she eventually brought about: the raising of the age of consent. Today there are many well-meaning but mistaken people, Christians among them, who would like to see that age lowered to fourteen.

In the *Daily Express* of January 31st 1976, John Braine wrote an article headed 'What age of consent?'. He said, by way of introduction,

'Two Home Office Committees are now debating whether the age of sexual consent should be lowered from sixteen. Pressure for reform is led by those who point out that almost 5,000 men were prosecuted for "unlawful sexual intercourse" during 1974—even though most of the young victims were consenting partners. Is this compatible with respect for the new law on sexual equality? In Victorian times a girl was allowed to say "yes" to sex at the amazingly early age of 12. Few parents today, no matter how modern, would support such an enormous step back. Most would ask, as the *Express* does now: "should we tamper with this law at all?" '

John Braine then pursues his argument quite properly and

forcefully against lowering the age of consent. I agree with every word he says. At the end of his article, the *Express* asks, 'Is John Braine's view too old-fashioned for the modern age? or is his the voice of sexual sanity?'

In 1972 Bishop John Robinson, as Chairman of the newly-formed Sexual Reform Society, gave a lecture to the Methodist Conference entitled 'The Place of Law in the Field of Sex'. In it he said: 'I think I am persuaded that probably the most realistic solution would be to lower the age of consent to fourteen so that no one having intercourse with a person above that age should automatically be committing a criminal offence.' I wrote my reply in a pamphlet in which I stated: 'With the full text of the lecture before me, I condemn this attitude especially in a priest and a bishop.' My 'Reply' was longer than John Braine's article but he touched all the arguments I put forward.

The ugly head of the Sexual Reform Society was raised again through a report of the 'Working Party on the Law in Relation to Sexual Behaviour'. The members who served on this working party were: The Rev. Lord Beaumont of Whitley, Miss Monica Furlong, Mr Antony Grey, Dr David Kerr, Mr John Lloyd Ely, QC, Mr C. H. Rolph, Mr Keith Wedmore, Dr D. J. West. Such a list might well have been balanced by an equal number of ordinary working people. This again would have meant a far greater simplification of the ground covered, since those actually appointed were from a class in a minority by far, and a class far superior in education and privilege. Further, the lowering of the age of consent would affect the masses far more than the children of those in the category covered by such a working party.

It is interesting to note that Dr Tony Smith said in a recent article in *The Times* on the subject of 'Separating the facts from opinions about promiscuity'. Speaking of research done by Mr Michael Schofield, he says: 'If anything the evidence suggests that further education leads to the questioning and rejection of traditional sexual morality.'

Christians today could learn much from Josephine Butler.

First and foremost there is her perfect example of complete trust and faith in God. Few can have done more for those who most needed care, and very few could have walked so closely with God to do it. She fought solidly for over twenty years against the greatest powers in the land, against Government itself. She gathered behind her the common people and used them for their own good. She braved the subtlest and most clever opposition. She championed the poor against the privileged. Her dedicated culture led privileged women to higher education. It also led the poorest and most ignorant women and girls to a position of dignity and decency. All generations could call her blessed. Do we really want to undo all the good she did by putting the clock back and lowering the age of consent?

Of legalised prostitution, Josephine wrote:

'Injustice is immoral, oppression is immoral, the sacrifice of the interests of the weaker to the stronger is immoral, and all these immoralities are embodied in all systems of legalised prostitution.'

The Times Home Affairs correspondent reported on February 25th 1976:

' "Sellers of contraceptives encourage children and young people to engage in sexual intercourse," the Responsible Society says in evidence to the Home Office Policy Committee inquiring into the law on sexual offences.

'The Society which represents doctors, teachers, parents and others concerned with the welfare of young people, says the age of consent for girls should be retained under the present law and not reduced.

'For increasing pressure on young people that encourages them to engage in sexual activities the Society blames the producers of trendy teen-age magazines, sellers of contraceptives, including F. C. Sales Ltd. "the commercial offshoot of the Family Planning Association", and some elements in the pop music industry that cultivate sexual mass hysteria.

'From 1966 to 1973 the incidence of gonorrhoea among girls under sixteen nearly trebled. In the same period illegitimate conceptions (births plus abortions) by girls under sixteen increased by nearly 300 per cent.

'The Society also says there should be no change in the present law of homosexual relationships. It adds that proposals by the Sexual Law Reform Society advocating an age of consent of 14 for boys and girls would be "licence for the paederast". The law governing incest should be retained.

Those people who wish to change the law by lowering the age of consent for girls have in mind love affairs with boys of similar age. Where consorting and co-habiting take place within the same age group, and it is seen not to be rape, little can be done about it and generally special consideration is given in the courts. Advice and guidance and care are uppermost in the minds of the authorities when dealing with such cases. But the great danger to young girls is from experienced men, old, middle-aged and younger, who deliberately seduce or rape. More serious still is the danger from those evil, vicious men who live wholly off the immoral earnings of young girls whom they procure and reduce by cruelty to near slavery. These are the worst offenders, for by them the girls are used for money-making alone.

In the spring of 1976, a BBC 'Man Alive' programme dealt with the age of consent. The doctors and social workers involved were chiefly concerned about the promiscuous activities of the young and the consequences. No mention at all was made of venereal disease and except for one passing reference by one of the men, nothing was said about the danger to young girls from vicious men. Nor, in letters to *The Times* and the like, do we find any deep concern about that vital matter, in spite of the fact that this is the reason for that particular law's existence.

Those who advocate the lowering of the age of consent are greatly lacking in understanding of the emotional make-up of normal young girls. We have all been moved by fairy stories about living happily ever after, and our elders loved to keep the fantasy alive as long as possible. Girls especially cherish the delightful picture of the ideal boy friend, dreaming of a lasting relationship. A breakdown of such a relationship is terribly serious to very great numbers of young girls. I have found that there is often a direct connection between this emotional condition and the prostitution scene.

Over the last twenty years I have met many prostitutes; they have been my friends. Although some of them went into prostitution out of loneliness, the great majority became involved as a result of disappointment and frustration. Having known the joy and excitement of a loving relationship, a girl expects that it will last. It is different for a boy. At its crudest, he has his fill of desire with the help of a girl who expects and behaves as if it must go on for ever. A boy's mother may urge him not to settle down because he is too young, which is often true. The girl feels unhappy and insecure, so that the boy begins to find her a bore, and inevitably a break comes about. Often she does not care what happens to her, and will run away from home. Out of sheer loneliness, and the need of somewhere to live, she becomes an easy prey for pimps and older prostitutes. Soon she is caught, without hope of escape. What is expected of her she has learned from her first sweet affair; but she is a long way from that now.

It was interesting to read, in *The Times* of June 29th 1976, the following passage under the headline, 'Casual Sex Acts "Can Lead to Misery" '. I quote it in full, because it endorses what I have said above, and have been saying for many years now.

'Casual sexual intercourse between teenagers of brief acquaintance can lead to misery, Dr James Hemming, the educational psychologist, writes in a new Family Doctor Booklet *Teenage Living and Loving.*

'Much unhappiness arises from the fact that physical desire alone may be a boy's chief reason for wanting intercourse, whereas the girl may think the boy's feelings are as romantically involved as hers are, Dr Hemming says.

'The reliable principle is: no making love without knowing well. "Then there is likely to be genuine feeling for one another and a real caring, without which sex can lead to misery instead of happiness."

'Whether a young couple decide to make love is a decision for them alone, but both should be well aware of what they are getting into and that sexual relationships bring a deep emotional involvement of much greater intensity than either may have expected.'

When a young girl has an affair with a grown man it is a different story and even more dangerous for the girl. Recently a schoolmaster was sent to prison for fifteen months for having unlawful intercourse with a girl of fourteen; he was thirty-six. He was 'infatuated' said a newspaper; and so, of course, was she, for she had attracted the attention and love of her teacher. She looked up to him; he fascinated her.

In a north country town a girl of nine was forced into prostitution by her sixteen-year-old brother. He supplied the men and they shared the money. The girl's friends of twelve and thirteen were having intercourse with men for sweets, clothes and money. Nine men aged between thirty-five and sixty-nine admitted intercourse with the girl. One was sent to prison for eighteen months; others were given suspended sentences.

The temptations are there; but for all the numbers of men brought to court there are very many more going free. The age of consent must be kept at sixteen to protect young girls against themselves and from the wiles of grown men. Children are easily beguiled and cheated. Prostitution reduces girls to the gutter while they are still young in years, yet already too old and wasted to be of any further use for 'the game' as it is so wrongly called.

The tragic picture drawn by Josephine Butler a century ago of sick, worn-out prostitutes is as true today. Helped perhaps more quickly downhill by drugs and drink and even methylated spirits, the end for these girls is hell on earth. It is the common end in my experience, and in trying to help them over many years, I have felt that the only hope of escape for them is to act when they are still young, or they will be lost for ever in degradation and wretchedness. Sickness and misery drive them to drink and despair when they are past attracting men. Obliged to become prostitutes' maids and to help to procure other young girls, they grow even more bitter. All the prostitutes I knew in my years in Stepney, with no exception, hated the life and themselves, but for the most part they were too deep in it ever to get out.

The battle which Josephine Butler fought and won a hundred years ago must be fought all over again today. I shall leave the final word with her:

> 'Never forget that if we allow persons belonging to any class of the citizens to be enslaved, however obscure, despised or degraded that class may be, these will not long continue to be the only slaves. The principle of individual liberty once infringed, will be gradually lost.'

Epilogue

A prayer to my adopted 'Saint' Josephine, who, over a hundred years ago, pioneered the kind of work now being done by the Wellclose Square Fund for the rescue and rehabilitation of young prostitutes and girls in moral danger.

JOSEPHINE, whose example in living witness to God was so perfect and whose humility gave the desire to kiss the feet of His Son, ceaselessly as did the prostitute sinner, and whose courageous spirit was the Spirit bequeathed us by the Master, let us graciously learn of you.

First let us love as you loved with your self-emptying devotion to the poorest and saddest of child prostitutes, beaten and used by cruel men. You gave them hospitality and shelter in your own home and ministered to them when dying and laid them to rest.

Give us your love, too, for those old and haggard women, still young in years, but broken by disease and weakness.

Grant to us, holy sister and patron, your fearlessness, equal as it was to all cunning and intrigue from the greatest and most powerful in the land; the devil's advocates in high office.

Give to us your love of home and family with your heartbreaks in suffering, with your gentleness in love and affection.

Give to us your knowledge and love and use of the Bible, and give to us the comfort and strength it gave to you.

Breathe in us your cleanness of heart and clarity of speaking and writing.

Give to us your eyes to see and appreciate the landscape and all art in nature.

Make us akin to your depth of understanding of people with patience. Give us your faith and your trust with steadfastness in all our dealings. Give us your honesty. Give us, too, your patriotism, love of country, with your hopes and prayers for leaders. Give us your character and singleness of heart. Finally, give us the breath of your absolute trust in God.

Bibliography

Josephine Butler, by E. Moberly Bell. Constable, 1962.

Josephine Butler and her Work for Social Purity, by M. Fawcett and E. M. Turner. Association for Social and Moral Hygiene (Josephine Butler Society), 1927.

Josephine Butler, an Autobiographical Memoir, ed. George W. Johnson and Lucy Johnson. Arrowsmith, Bristol, 1912.

A Singular Iniquity: The Campaigns of Josephine Butler, by Glen Petrie. Macmillan, 1971.

The Age of Consent, by Ann Stafford. Hodder and Stoughton, 1964.

Recollections of George Butler by his wife, by Josephine Butler. Arrowsmith, Bristol.

The Noble Women of the Staircase and Atrium Windows in the Lady Chapel, Liverpool Cathedral. Sermons by the Rev. William McNeill. *Liverpool Daily Post.*

Also papers and periodicals lent by Miss Hetha Butler.

"FATHER JOE"

The Autobiography of Joseph Williamson of Poplar and Stepney is still available from the author.